SWING TRADING

HOW TO SWING TRADE FROM A-Z
7-DAY CRASH COURSE FOR BEGINNERS
STRATEGIES TO TRADE OPTIONS, STOCKS AND FOREX
SECRET STRATEGIES, TIPS AND TRICKS

MARK STOCK

Table of Contents

Introduction

Swing trading is an exciting opportunity for small and individual investors to make an income on the stock market. In fact, swing trading is a general technique that can be used to earn income from stocks, commodities, and even on Forex.

You can think of swing trading as a middle ground between long term investing and day trading. We will explore the similarities and differences along with specific details in the book, but, for now, you can think of swing trading as day trading but over longer time frames and with far less risk. Rather than trying to make money off of your trades in the matter of a few hours, with swing trading your goal is to make money off changing share prices over time frames ranging from days to many weeks.

A swing trader doesn't need to sit at his computer watching the stock markets all day long, although you certainly can if that is an option for you and you like doing it. Swing traders can also start small and grow their business over time. Day trading involves lots of upfront costs instead.

The word "business" should catch your eye. In short, swing trading is a business. Rather than building a long-term retirement account, swing trading is all about earning profits in the short term. While substantial profits are possible, it's not a get-rich-quick scheme and although it can be done on a part-time basis, we want you to start thinking of swing trading as a business from this point forward. The goal is to earn profits, and you can use those profits as ordinary income if you like or reinvest them to build your retirement account or some combination of the two. That is entirely up to you. But keep in mind one thing: very few people are going to make a million bucks in their first year and go right into retirement.

That said, swing trading can be a very lucrative way to make a living, and if you are interested in business and finance, it can be a lot of fun! In order to get there, you are going to have to study and become an expert in the field. The journey can start with this book. Let's get started!

Chapter 1: What is Swing Trading?

In this first chapter, we are going to introduce the concept of swing trading. It's essential to distinguish swing trading from other common methods of trading and investing and you also need to know what the requirements for entry are. After introducing the concept of swing trading, we will explore how swing trading differs from day trading and also how it differs from long-term or buy and hold investing. We will also explore the question of who is best suited for swing trading. Before you start, you need to know if this is something that would be good for you and your financial situation. We will do that in the chapter with a discussion of the tax implications of swing trading.

What is swing trading?

The concept of swing trading is deceptively simple. All it means is that you buy and sell stocks or other investments to make short-term profits. In other words, swing trading seeks to profit from short-term price movements on the stock market (or other markets such as currency trading). However, unlike day trading, the price movements we are interested in last from days to weeks or possibly up to a couple of months or so.

It differs from day trading in one key aspect. Swing trading involves holding securities overnight, possibly for weeks at a time. Therefore, you can be looking for short-term swings in the price of a stock, for example. However, you aren't looking for that swing in price to occur over the course of a single day, but rather over a few days, or weeks. Some people who swing trade can even lengthen that time period out to a couple of months or so. You might even say you are a swing trader if your strategy is to hold stocks for several months, but buy low and sell high over that period.

As you might guess, the level of involvement and stress in swing trading is lower than what you would find with day trading. We are going to explore the differences between swing trading and day trading in detail in a later section. Nevertheless, generally speaking, it's going to involve less upfront capital and a lower level of involvement in the daily movements of stocks or whatever market you are involved with. Swing trading can be used on stocks, Forex, commodities, and even with crypto currencies. However, for the purposes of this book, we will generally focus on the stock market. The principles are the same no matter what you trade.

Where can you use swing trading?
Swing trading can be used in virtually any market. It's a technique, rather than something specialized for a specific market like crypto currency. Nevertheless, swing traders primarily trade on stock markets. But you can use swing trading

as a technique when trading commodities, currencies, and anything else that will see price swings up-and-down over the time periods of interest, and that means you could apply swing trading to anything that gets traded. You could even think of trading options as a form of swing trading since you're hoping to profit on the same moves of the stock, although options are quite a different ball game overall.

Our focus in this book is going to be on stock trading. But keep in mind that you could use the exact same techniques, including the methods of analysis for the most part on currency markets as well.

How does swing trading differ from day trading?

Firstly, let's make an observation. You cannot day trade without making it a full-time living. Starting from some first principles, a day trade is one that opens and closes the position on the same day. You might only hold the stock for a few hours or even for a matter of minutes.

From this definition, you can understand that you need to be paying strict attention to the movements of the stock or security on a moment-by-moment basis. The first thing you do with day trading is you need to know the exact right moment to buy the stock. Of course, there are high odds that you will guess wrong (not that day traders "guess"). But what's working against you is that over the short term, although traders do utilize a lot of analysis in their work, the stock market is essentially a chaotic system, with a lot of randomness built into it.

Secondly, there is the problem of what is the right moment to sell. Therefore, you are going to need to know when to get out of the position at just the right time so that you're exiting and able to make good profits. That is a very tough and nerve-racking game to play.

Of course, there are many good methods that, if followed to the letter, can produce success in day trading. That is not something anyone is going to do on the fly and be successful at. There may be that one person in a thousand that can do that, but most people are going to need extensive training. Even then, the reality is that most day traders fail to make consistent profits, or even profit at all.

With swing trading, you're looking to profit on price moves, but it's a far more relaxed method. If things are not working out for you on any given day, you can wait it out.

Another important difference between day trading and swing trading is that day trading has substantial capital requirements up front. In order to be a day trader, the vast majority of brokerages are going to require that you have $25,000 in your account. That doesn't necessarily have to be $25,000 in cash; it could be a $25,000 combination of cash and stocks. That said, it's a significant barrier to entry for many people. Even people who have $25,000 on hand may not want to risk it all on a few day trades.

There are a couple of brokerages that don't have this requirement, and they allow you to day trade with any amount of funds. However, they charge massive commissions. Those may be suitable to learn on, and you can even profit. But professional traders don't use them because of the high commissions, and you probably wouldn't want to stick with them long term if you find out you have a knack for day trading and can make profits from it.

Day trading as a defined category goes well beyond what brokerages think; it's a matter of law and even taxes. There are strict legal definitions that were created by the United States government that say exactly what a day trader is. The first part of the definition to be aware of is that you are going to be labeled a day trader if you enter into four-day trades within any five-day period. Just to be clear, a day trade is defined as buying and selling the same security on the same trading day.

Also, keep in mind the five-day period does not end at the weekend or include weekends. Therefore, it's any five consecutive business days. Alternatively, as they say in the business, five consecutive trading days.

A swing trader, in contrast, is someone that is going to hold the position at least overnight. In fact, swing traders may hold a position for several days, weeks, and even out to a few months in time. A swing trader simply holds his positions for a far longer amount of time than a day trader does.

Secondly, there are no capital requirements imposed on swing traders. If you have five dollars in your account and buy a share of a stock that is five dollars a share, you can swing trade that one share of stock. The only requirement for swing trading is that you have the capital available that you need for your own personal goals (and any requirements that your broker has to open an account, if any). Of course, buying one share of a five dollar stock isn't going to get you anywhere financially, but the point is swing trading isn't really an official designation to the point that day trading is. As far as the broker is concerned, a swing trader isn't any different from any other investor.

When you are buying a stock traditionally, as we will see in the next section, you will do so based on the *fundamentals* of the company. What that means, in a nutshell, is that you're going to be looking at the recent history of revenues and profits ("recent" being over the past five years), the management team, price to earnings ratio and whether or not the stock is undervalued. You would also be looking at the company's long-term prospects, as well as its history. What are the products it is coming out with? Is it engaged in R&D? Will it be expanding into new markets? Fundamentals mean looking at something for long-term investment and really getting into the business that the company is engaged in.

Day traders are not concerned with the fundamentals of a company. That could come into play at times, like on a day when a company has an earnings call. For a day trader, the concern is based on how the stock is moving over a few minutes or hours. This fact may have absolutely nothing to do with fundamentals or, as our example of an earnings call illustrates, it could be related to it. The point is: fundamentals are of prime concern for long-term investors, but it's a tangential or fleeting issue for day traders.

Day trading moves might be based on euphoria or panic of people trading at the moment. How many times have you seen the market go up or down based on a news story? Those changes are usually fleeting, but day traders seek to profit from them.

Day trades could be based on the release of a new product or some other short-term event that drives the share price up. There are many reasons and to be honest as a day trader in many cases, you don't even have to care what the reasons are. Instead, you're just looking at the charts and so forth to spot a short-term move in the stock price, either up or down. The techniques of analyzing the charts and data in the stock market to spot a possible short term move up or down and share price is called *technical analysis.* Long-term investors don't pay attention to that at all. As far as a long-term investor is concerned, technical analysis may not even exist. Swing traders, however, need to understand technical analysis, although they don't have to be the experts at it that day traders have to be.

So, in short, a swing trader kind of takes a middle ground between the two extremes of day trading and long-term investing. As a swing trader, you will be paying attention to technical analysis, but it won't take as central a role as it does in day trading. Secondly, while day traders pay relatively little attention to fundamental analysis, generally speaking, a swing trader is going to be much more interested in the fundamentals of the company. But not quite as focused as a Warren Buffett who looks at long time horizons.

Who is swing trading suitable for?

With the previous thoughts in mind, it should be clear that a day trader is going to be working on trading full-time. There really isn't an option to be a part-time day trader if you expect to make consistent profits. Of course, people might get lucky from time to time buying low and selling high on the same day, but to make consistent earnings you need to be doing live technical analysis and constantly follow financial news. It's a full-time job.

In contrast, it is possible to be a part-time swing trader. Swing trading can be suitable for people who have a full-time job they don't want to give up, and as a result, can't day trade as a practical matter. That said, swing trading is also suitable for people who actually want to do it full-time. So, it's actually a more flexible approach to trading in general.

One of the differences between swing trading and day trading is that swing trading is something that can be used by people who don't have much time to devote to following the markets and financial news. That said, you still have to pay attention to those things. A passion for the stock markets in financial news and business is something that a swing trader will need.

Swing trading and day trading also carry different levels of risk, something that needs to be emphasized a lot. Let's be clear – like any trading or investment, swing trading carries risk. Overall, it's a lower risk as compared to day trading.

Let's sum it up. A day trader is somebody who's going to enter into multiple trades on the same day. At the very minimum, the day trader is going to buy and sell a security on the same day, which would be *two* trades. Day traders do not hold positions overnight.

The primary analysis tools used for day trading are technical tools. These will include charts, candles, and moving averages that can tell a day trader where herd behavior among traders is heading. Day trading requires an advanced understanding of technical analysis. If you aren't sure what technical analysis is, don't worry, we will be talking about it in this book.

Fundamentals can be a concern for the day trader, but not necessarily. A day trader will buy stock in a company with horrible fundamentals if they think the company is going to have a short-term rise in share price they can profit from. Alternatively, they could short the stock; something long-term buy-and-hold investors aren't interested in doing.

Remember also that a day trader must have $25,000 in his or her account, something that isn't required for anyone else. Significant losses are possible, and it's generally considered that you have a loss potential of up to 100% of your capital.

Of course, a smart trader is going to use techniques like stop-loss orders to mitigate losses, which we will talk about in this book.

Swing trading, in contrast, doesn't require a full-time commitment or the investment of large amounts of capital to get started. So, you can start with small amounts of upfront money and do it on a part-time basis. Swing trading also combines fundamental and technical analysis at a far greater degree than day trading usually does. Although you won't do it to the extent that Warren Buffett would, you are going to be paying attention to the fundamentals of the companies you invest in. Think about it – is a stock going to rise over the course of a few months for a company that doesn't have some good fundamentals? Probably not.

Overall, swing trading is a far more flexible approach. You can do it part-time or full-time, with small amounts of money up front or by investing large amounts of money. You can gradually grow it over time, starting out small and working up to a larger account and engaging in larger trades as time goes on. Finally, relatively speaking, the risk is lower.

How Does Swing Trading Differ from Buy and Hold Investing?

Most people come to the stock market thinking about traditional buy-and-hold investing. Buy-and-hold investing is a technique that is focused on the long-term gains of the stock market and highly valued companies.

If you invest in specific companies at all, and many people don't, a buy-and-hold investor is looking for high-quality buys. It's true investing, meaning that you're focused on the fundamentals of the company and its long-term prospects, and you are putting your money into the market to invest in the company over the long-term, which can mean up to 30 years or more.

The buy-and-hold investor is going to dig into a company very deeply when it comes to the fundamentals. That means going over the financial statements and cash flow in detail, seeing how things are changing year to year, and reading all the earnings reports and following the calls. It also means studying the management team, including who they are and what is in their backgrounds. You are going to familiarize yourself with the company's products and what markets they are in.

A good buy-and-hold investor that invests in specific companies will approach it as if a friend or relative said: "hey do you want to invest in my business?" Buy-and-hold investors have low turnover rates in their portfolios. Some buy-and-hold investors are actually income or dividend investors, hoping to make a living off dividend payments either now or in the future, while safely preserving their capital. They may be inclined to invest in a slowly changing stock like Chevron or IBM, as opposed to some stock that sees significant price swings over days, weeks, or months.

Many buy-and-hold investors these days don't even invest in individual companies. With the advent of exchange-traded funds, it's possible to buy and sell shares on the stock market while investing in index funds rather than investing in individual companies or being constrained by stodgy and expensive mutual funds. Given that an index like the S&P 500 is going to go up over the long term barring some unforeseen disaster, a simple buying and hold strategy is to load up on index funds like SPY. Of course, the most extreme buy-and-hold investor would be someone who invests in mutual funds, and they let the fund manager keep track of all the investments and rarely check on it themselves. Such investors just hope to have a "nest egg" in retirement.

Regardless of whether a buy-and-hold or long-term investor invests in specific companies, index funds, mutual funds, or some combination out of all of these, they will use the same basic techniques. Those techniques involve *diversification* of your portfolio and using methods like *dollar cost averaging*. They will also be looking for so-called value stocks, which are undervalued at the present time based on the fundamentals of the company, and so the investor hopes to make cheap buys of quality stocks that will appreciate over the long term.

We see that, right off the bat, buy-and-hold investing is quite different from swing trading. Swing trading does pay some attention to the fundamentals of the company, but the focus remains on short-term profits. Even when looking at fundamentals, the swing trader is interested in how they are going to impact share prices in the coming weeks, not over the course of decades.

Techniques like diversification are of limited interest to the swing trader. You will have a little bit of diversity in that, you are going to be buying and selling multiple securities over time as you get involved with more trades simultaneously. Beginning swing traders may not have any diversity at all and may only be buying and selling one security at a time.

Dollar cost averaging is obviously not something a swing trader would consider at all. If you don't know what that means, dollar cost averaging is a strategy that uses investing at regular intervals. The idea is to average out the price paid for shares of stock as it fluctuates up and down. People who use dollar cost averaging have a philosophy that over the long term, those price fluctuations are going to average out, and many believe you can't predict price fluctuations anyway (they might take a dim view of technical analysis).

The concept of Dollar cost averaging does not enter the mindset of the swing trader at all.

Furthermore, a long-term or a buy-and-hold investor is not interested in generating immediate income from their investments for the most part. Some will hope to generate income from dividend investments. However, even most dividend investors (unless they are already retired or have huge amounts of capital in the stock market) are going to reinvest any income generated from dividends into new shares. This is done in the hopes of generating more long-term wealth over multiple decades.

To summarize, a buy-and-hold investment strategy is one that is based on long-term wealth building and wealth preservation. It relies on diversification, analysis of fundamentals, and dollar cost averaging and reinvestment as its primary strategies.

In contrast, swing trading looks to generate an income *now*, or at least over the course of months, rather than years or decades. Although they will rely to a certain extent on fundamentals, that plays a smaller role for the swing trader. The swing trader also uses technical analysis that is used by the day trader in order to estimate how the price of a stock is going to change in the near future. A buy-and-hold investor does not pay attention to technical analysis at all.

Tax implications

If you are trading for income, there can be significant tax implications. First of all, keep in mind that when you buy and sell shares of stock (or any other asset), you can incur capital gains or losses. These have tax implications, and tax law distinguishes between long-term capital gains and short-term capital gains. Any investment held for a year or longer generates long-term capital gains as far as the IRS is concerned. In that case, the tax treatment is quite favorable. Depending on the amount of money we are talking about, the tax rate can range between 0-20%. In the upper-income tax brackets, a 20% tax rate is quite favorable.

Short term profits aren't viewed as favorably, so any capital gain that takes place over a time period of less than a year is considered to be a short-term capital gain, and that is something that would be taxed as ordinary income. If you are a swing trader, for the most part, that is how your earnings are going to be taxed. As a swing trader, most of your trades are going to be taking place over time frames of days or weeks. If you make enough money to get into the top tax bracket, before considering possible deductions, you're going to be looking at the 37% tax rate.

For day traders, there are actually some important tax benefits. Without getting into the details, be aware that under some circumstances day traders can deduct all of their losses on their taxes. This is opposed to ordinary schedule C business, which limits how much the losses can be applied to deductions. Day traders can also deduct items like financial news subscriptions which are considered expenses related to their business. This is not an advantage that is generally available to others, but under certain circumstances, swing traders can take advantage of this tax loophole (if you want to call it that). We aren't here to give advice on taxes, so that is something you will have to work out with a tax advisor or an accountant. However, it's something to be aware of as a possibility. You probably won't know how it's going to work out for you until the year is done and the accountant can go over all of your trades and expenses related to the business.

Speculation versus Investment

Are you a speculator or a swing trader? Simply put, a speculator is someone that hopes to make money from appreciating prices of an asset. In the case of the stock market, you can short stocks or buy put options and make money off short-term price declines of an asset. In any case, speculation is distinct from investment.

The latter means that you're putting money behind a company, product, or idea hoping that it is profitable over the long term. You may even be beholden to the company or emotionally attached to its products, or simply believe in the products it is making for many reasons. Many people are huge fans of Apple, for example, and so would be perfectly happy putting large amounts of money in Apple stock and leaving it there for unlimited amounts of time. They would do so because they believe in the long-term prospects of the company and the products it makes.

Another example might be Tesla. If you are a big fan of electric cars, you might put money into Tesla because you believe in the company's mission, and you might think that is the future of transportation.

A speculator, in contrast, is someone who hopes to buy low and sell high at the moment. You could even buy the same stocks as the investor. So, if Apple had an earnings call the next day, you might buy shares of Apple because the rumors are it's going to be a real positive call, so that is going to drive up the share price. Then as soon as share prices jump, you sell your shares in Apple.

Speculators are often associated with booms and busts. Speculators reigned supreme during the California gold rush, buying and selling gold and interests in gold mines in the hope of earning quick money. That speculation role in gold has always existed and continues to exist; many people bought and sold gold over short time periods in the late 1970s when the price was skyrocketing.

Perhaps the easiest way to understand investment versus speculation is to think about real estate. An investor in real estate could, for example, purchase homes over time to rent out. The goal of the investor would be to accumulate assets and hence build wealth, by accumulating a number of homes over the decades. They also seek to derive regular income from the homes in the rents paid, after the mortgages for the homes have been paid off. Moreover, the investor may hope at some point in the future to sell the homes to make profits, but they won't be looking to do that until decades later, if ever.

In contrast, a speculator in real estate would hope to buy and sell homes at a quick profit over short time periods. In recent years, the most famous real estate speculators were home flippers. They would buy a bargain, a decently sized home in a decent neighborhood that was a "fixer-upper," remodel the house and then sell it within a few months at a hefty profit. Of course, implicit in this process is their attempt to not only profit of the improvements they make to the home, but they are also attempting to profit on the steadily increasing prices of homes and real estate in general. Of course, in 2008, we found out that this doesn't always work.

Swing trading is considered a form of speculation. Traders use swing trading for the sole purpose of profiting from the appreciating price of the asset, and that is speculation.

It's not a matter of whether or not speculation is a good or bad thing. Some people have a taste for it, and some people don't. There are many people like Warren Buffett that even look down on speculation, but what he thinks or doesn't think isn't of any relevance here. You should be aware that speculation does carry more risk than investing. When you speculate, it's inevitable that sometimes your trades are going to be losers.

Before you launch a swing trading career, determining whether you are comfortable with swing trading, rather than investing for the good of the company and long-term prospects, is going to be something that you are going to have to think about and consider carefully.

Now let's start looking at some of the general ways that swing trading is carried out and what you will be looking for.

Swing trading in a nutshell

When you are engaged in swing trading, you are going to look at buying shares of stock when you believe they are at a relatively low position. This could happen for multiple reasons. For example, it could be the case that shares of stock have dropped in price because there has been a recent selloff. This happens all the time, and there are often market panics over fleeting news items or a remark that President Trump made. You should always see such downturns as a buying opportunity. Whether the markets go back up in a day or a few weeks or even months matters not to the swing trader. The one certainty is that when stocks drop because of a massive sell-off, they will go back up. The key is knowing when the best time to buy is so that you can maximize your profits later.

There could be other reasons to expect a price swing. For example, there may be an upcoming earnings report. That can be something that could go one way or the other, which means you'll have to be carefully studying the financial news to have an idea of what is going on. For example, Tesla may be about to announce that they are going to be able to ramp up production of the Model 3. This could represent a buying opportunity if you get a hold of your shares before the announcement is officially made. Therefore, you could buy shares a week or two before the announcement. Then when it is official, you can be reasonably certain that the share price is going to rise substantially. Then when it does, you sell your shares and book your profits.

Of course, there is an inherent risk – the announcement might go the other way instead, which could mean heavy losses. As we'll see, you should protect yourself with stop-loss orders to prevent massive wipeouts. However, the swing trader isn't as impacted by changes as the day trader is. Remember that you can hold your position for as long as you like. So another strategy in response to a trade that doesn't work out – provided that you are able to tie up the capital and have other capital to work with in getting into other trades – is to simply hold on and wait for other factors to cause a favorable price move.

As we mentioned in the first chapter, there isn't any official rule for time frames used in swing trading. You can enter into a trade, hoping that the price is going to move high enough to make substantial profits in a matter of days. Or it may be a week or several weeks before you end up selling your shares. It could even be six or nine months. It's entirely up to you, and it's a far more flexible way of trading than day trading.

However, one important consideration is that you're not doing your trades randomly. So, you aren't going to load up on shares of a specific company and then hope they increase at some point and call that 'swing trading.' With swing trading, you are going to enter into a certain trade because you have done the analysis and believe that the share price is at a relative low, and your analysis tells you that in the coming days, weeks, or months, the share price is going to see a substantial rise.

Can you swing trade index funds?

The answer is definitely yes. Many index funds track virtually everything, from the S & P 500 to emerging markets to REITs. In this case, we are talking about exchange-traded funds. Moreover, exchange-traded fund or ETF as they are known is traded on the stock market, but it's a pooled investment like a mutual fund. You are not going to swing trade mutual funds; they have high expenses and only trade once a day, so as a swing trader it is not something you are going to be interested in at all. Nevertheless, exchange-traded funds are an entirely different ball game even though there are many similarities. For our purposes, the only things that are important about exchange-traded funds are that they trade like stocks on stock-market exchanges and that many of them are subject to wild price swings. One that may be of interest to you is SPY – an ETF that tracks the S & P 500. You can also look at DIA, an ETF that tracks the Dow Jones Industrial Average. As you know, the Dow Jones and S & P 500 can go through significant price movements based on what happens in the news. You can pay attention to things like upcoming jobs reports, GDP growth, and trade deals. Political events and terrorist attacks can also have a big influence on these indexes.

That means if you are going to utilize them in your swing trading, you need to be paying close attention to financial, economic, and political news. One tweet from the President can send the markets down fast or make them rise just as fast. So next time the President issues a tweet, keep in mind that could be a major buying opportunity for SPY or DIA.

The techniques here would be the same, even though the influences are more of general sentiment rather than paying attention to a specific stock and what a company is doing. Over time, the indexes move upwards, that is just a historical fact. But they can also swing up and down quite a bit over shorter time periods. So, look for buying opportunities first, bad news that causes them to dip. Then you can buy shares and then be prepared to sell them. Your selling position may simply be a goal that is gradually reached as the stock market inevitably goes up as time passes or it might happen when good news suddenly hits, such as breaking news that GDP growth was over 3%. At that point, you unload your shares and take the profits. Of course, the next time bad news hits and the indexes crash again, that's going to be another buying opportunity.

Clear goals, limit orders, and stop-loss orders
Most people go into the stock market without having clear, specific goals in mind. They just hope to make money. That is not a successful approach for a swing trader. As a swing trader, you

need to have specific, clearly delimited goals in mind. That means not letting emotions take over.

Suppose, for the sake of example, that you have purchased 1,000 shares of SPY at $288 per share. Your goal might be to make $4 per share. In the event that it drops to $286 per share, you might want to exit the position out of concern that further losses would be more than you would willingly accept and you also want to exit the position so that you could put the capital to work somewhere else.

Leaving this to fate is a bad idea. Most people place what is known as market orders on their trades. Therefore, you simply sell your shares at the prevailing market price. Doing this while swing trading is going to require that you manually take action when you reach your goals. That, of course, can be a problem because you might start getting excited over a rise in share price, having visions of dancing dollar bills as the profits come in. The risk here is that you will wait too long to exit the position, and the share price will drop wiping out even minimal profits.

That's why you need to set specific price boundaries for your buying and selling of the shares. In addition, it is better to have them automatically enforced. In the case of selling at a profit, you can place what's called a limit order. A limit order means you specify the price you're willing to accept, but the sale of the shares won't actually happen unless and until the share price reaches that level. In our example, you could place a limit order of $292 for the SPY to sell it. A limit order can be used to buy or sell a given stock at the specified price or higher. So, in this example, if the share price rises to $292 or better, then your shares will be sold automatically, and the proceeds will be credited to your account.

Keep in mind that if the price doesn't go to $292 or higher, your limit order would never be executed. If you wanted to exit the trade, you could cancel the order and sell at the current market price. So maybe SPY goes to $290, and that is not as much as you hoped, but its languishing with no near-term indication of an upward trend in price. You could cancel your limit order and place a market order just to sell the shares and take the smaller level of profits.

You could also place a stop loss order, which is essentially a limit order to sell the shares if the price drops to a certain point or lower. Therefore, in this case, you could place an order to sell the shares if the price dropped to $286. If that happened, the sale would occur automatically. That would protect you from the catastrophic result of a massive sell-off that sends the share price crashing.

The 1% Rule

Financial advisors suggest that you only risk 1-2% of your account on a single trade. If you have a $50,000 account, that means only risking $500 to $1,000 on a single trade. What this does not mean is that you would only buy $500-$1,000 worth of shares; it means that you use a stop loss order to limit potential losses, and the number of losses would be limited to $500-$1,000.

As a simple example, if you limit your losses per trade to 1% on a $50,000 account, that means a maximum of a $500 loss. You can decide how much per share you are willing to lose to determine how many shares you can buy. If we decide we can lose $0.50 per share, then that would mean we could buy $500/$0.50 = 1,000 shares. Of course: you have to be able to afford the 1,000 shares. AMD is trading at $32 a share, so we could buy 1,000 shares for $32,000, and place a stop loss at $31.50 per share, which means the shares will be sold automatically if the price drops to that price point.

Of course, there are risks involved, the share price could drop to $30 a share and then rebound later to $34 a share, and since you had that stop loss in place, then you would miss out on that particular price movement.

Let's return to our example of SPY, with a potential loss of $2 per share (buying the shares at $288 per share and selling them at

33

$286 per share with a stop loss order) then, using the 1% rule, that would enable us to purchase $500/$2 = 250 shares. Using a 2% threshold, that means we could risk $1,000/$2 = 500 shares. Unfortunately, either one entails more money than we have in our account at $288 per share, so we'll have to go with a different scenario. We could raise the possible loss per share we are willing to accept to $3 a share. This means we could buy $500/$3 = 167 shares. The cost at $288 a share would be $48,096, nearly our entire account. Nevertheless, if you are expecting big news, or you're getting in early after big news already came out, it might be worth it.

First, let us look at what happens if we lose out, and the share price ended up dipping to $285 a share. In that case, if we placed a stop-loss order, it would be executed. We'd lose $3 a share for a total of $3 x 167 = $501. The sale would generate 167 shares x $285/share = $47,595 that we would have back in our account for use with other trades. If the share price kept dropping, say to $279 a share, we would breathe a sigh of relief knowing that we had protected our principal, for the most part, taking what is really a small loss at $501. If we had waited until the shares dropped to $279, we would end up selling for $46,593, resulting in a much larger loss of capital of $1,503. You can see how a stop loss can protect you from large losses.

This is more important for swing traders, actually. As a swing trader, you might not be in front of the computer all day. If you are a part-time trader, you might be in a meeting at work when the price drops to $279 per share, or even lower. Therefore, you would have missed the opportunity to sell off the shares manually or you might be taking a shower. Things can happen fast on the stock market, and it is best to protect yourself using pre-determined boundaries that are acceptable rather than changing it. Also, note that people can have their judgment clouded when prices are dropping. If you were lucky enough to be at your computer, you might hold on at $279 a share, convincing yourself that it's got to go up soon, since it was $288 a share just a day or two ago. What happens if instead it drops to $275 a share and stays there?

On the upper end, if we bought 167 shares and the price ended up going to $293, but we sold at $292, then we'd have 167 shares x $292/share = $48,764. So, we'd profit by $668.

The point of this exercise isn't to focus on the specific numbers – rather, you should focus on the mindset and actions taken. These are the mindset and actions that a successful swing trader will rely on. Always protect yourself from massive losses by using a stop loss order and be disciplined in selling your shares and taking realizable profits rather than waiting too long, when things often decline again in nearly inevitable fashion.

Use analysis like this to set upper and lower bounds you are willing to accept on each trade.

Chapter 2: Candles and Candlestick Charts

Before you understand how to read charts properly for the purpose of swing trading, it's crucial to understand candlesticks or candles for short. If you haven't used candles before, you can add them to any stock chart provided by websites that have stock charts. They aren't typically shown on the news because a simple line chart is easier to understand, and candles are a little bit more technical. However, candles are actually fairly easy to understand.

Candles were developed by Japanese rice traders to help them understand price trends. They show the volume of trading, the high price, low price, and open and closing prices. A candle represents a specific time frame, which can be varied, so, for example, you can have one-day candles. In that case, the candle would represent the day's high price, low price, open price, and closing price. However, you can have candles over short time periods like one hour, or five minutes, or even one minute. In the case of one hour then, the candle would represent the price at the start of the hour (open), the price at the end of the hour (close), the volume of trading for that hour, and the high and low prices reached during the hour. Day traders would be interested in candles for 1 minute, 5 minutes, or 1-hour intervals, as a swing trader at the most you are going to be looking at single day price swings.

Structure of a candlestick

On color charts (which are virtually all stock charts these days), candles are colored red or green. The candlestick has two wicks, sticking out from a body. The size of the body indicates the volume of trading. As we will see, the volume is an important indicator to look at as a swing trader, not just the price. The wicks that stick out of the candle indicate the high and low prices of the trading period. A candle can be bullish, meaning that over the time period of interest, the price of the stock went up. On the other hand, the candle can be bearish; indicating that over the time period in question, the price of the stock went down.

A green candle is bullish, indicating that prices are rising. As a result, the bottom of the candle indicates the opening price, and the top of the candle indicates the closing price. A red candle is bearish so that the top of the candle represents the opening price, and the bottom of the candle represents the closing price. The following picture illustrates the basics of candlesticks:

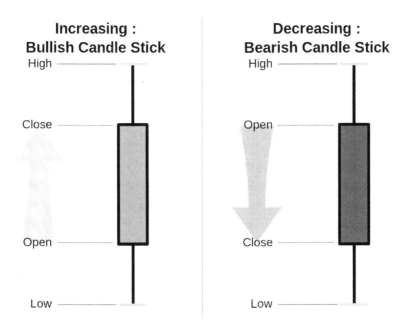

Picture 1

In the event you come across a black and white chart, a bearish candlestick will be solid black, and a bullish candlestick will be white in the center, but with a black outline. The lines sticking out from the candle body are sometimes called wicks but are also known as shadows.

There are many different candlesticks that you can read on charts, which are taken to be indicators of coming trends. Obviously, this doesn't always work, but as a swing trader, it is essential that you understand how to recognize different candlesticks. Now that you understand the basic characteristics of candlesticks, let's review the main types and things you want to look for in candlestick charts.

Bullish Hammer and Inverted Hammer

The main thing you are going to use candlesticks for is to find signals that indicate a trend reversal. A hammer forms when you have a candlestick that looks pretty much like a cartoon hammer, so you will have a small body, with one small wick coming out of one end and a very long wick coming out the other end. This close up from a Tesla chart shows a bullish hammer (circled in the dotted line oval):

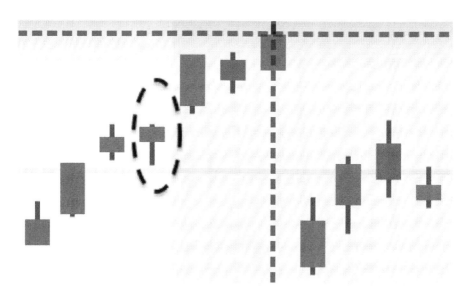

Picture 2

40

Generally speaking, this can indicate a coming price reversal when you see it as part of a downtrend. The long lower wick indicates that sellers drove the price down over the trading period. However, the short body indicates that, at the end of the period, the closing price was higher, meaning that bullish traders drove the price back up at the end of the trading period. Remember that the closing price is the top of the candlestick body, so in the example shown- the hammer is green – indicating that the closing price was higher than the day's low price by a large margin and it was also higher than the opening price for the trading period.

On the far left and right of the diagram, you see two more hammers, but they are upside down. These are called inverted hammers. That indicates that the closing price was quite a bit lower than the periods high, meaning that there was some selling pressure during the time period. However, the closing price was still higher than the opening price for the period, so it's still a bullish candlestick, which could indicate a trend reversal. In fact, the one on the left did represent a trend reversal.

To have a genuine hammer or inverted hammer, the long wick should be twice as long as or longer than the body. Nevertheless, you can generally eyeball them on candlestick charts.

Bearish Inverted Hammer and Shooting Star

A red inverted hammer happens when the open price, closing price, and low price of the time period are relatively close in value, but the closing price was lower than the opening price, and there was an extremely high price over the time period. If an inverted hammer occurs at the top of an uptrend, it's called a shooting star. The long wick indicates that buyers drove prices up during the time period, but the lower closing price indicates that sellers drove prices down by closing. If you see an inverted hammer (shooting star) at the top of an uptrend, this can indicate a coming downtrend. Here you can see an illustration of a shooting star at the top of an uptrend followed by a downtrend for SNAP.

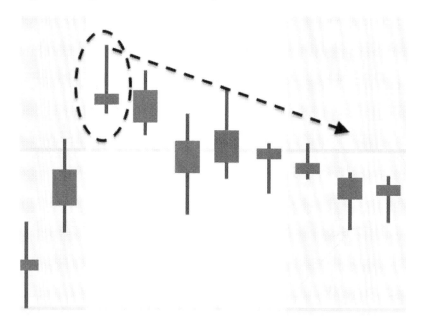

Picture 3

Engulfing Candle

When the body of one color of the candle is much larger than the preceding, opposite colored candle, we say that it is an engulfing pattern. This can be an indication of a coming reversal because a large candlestick body indicates a large trading volume. If the candlestick is green, that means there was a large trading volume with a closing price that was higher than the opening price, and so it is bullish, possibly indicating a reversal if it occurs at the bottom of a downtrend.

In the image below, a green or bullish candlestick clearly engulfs the red or bearish candlestick to its left. That can indicate a reversal into an uptrend but look for this pattern when stock prices have been decreasing.

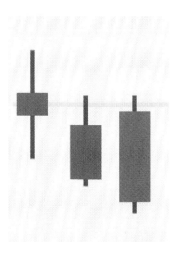

Picture 4

At the top of an uptrend, it can be a sign of reversal into a downtrend if a red or bearish candle engulfs the bullish candle to its left. This is a very serious engulfing candle:

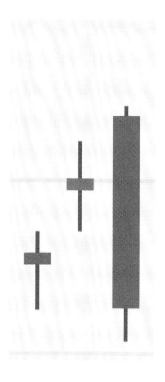

Picture 5

Doji

The "doji" has a narrow candlestick body. That indicates that there is indecision between sellers and buyers, or bears and bulls if you want to call them that. The meaning of the doji is that for the given time period, the opening and closing prices were about the same. The wicks on a doji can be long or short but are about the same length. If found at the top or bottom of a trend, it could mean a reversal is coming.

Picture 6

Morning Star

A morning star pattern is a strong trend reversal signal. A bearish candlestick with a large body is followed by a bullish doji, which is followed by an engulfing bullish candle (image by Commontrader, for Wikipedia):

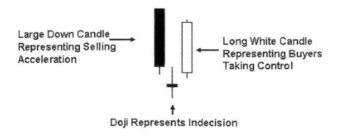

Picture 7

When everything is reversed, it's called an evening star.

Three White Soldiers

Three bullish candlesticks in a row coming out of a downtrend is a strong uptrend signal. Likewise, three red soldiers (bearish) at the top of an uptrend is a signal of a coming downtrend. The example below shows three bullish candlesticks in a row.

Picture 8

Piercing Line

In this trend indicator, a bullish candle that had a lower opening price follows a bearish candle. That means the bottom of the green or bullish candle is going to be lower on the chart. It's a bullish signal because it indicates that despite the lower open, the bullish traders were able to push the price up by closing.

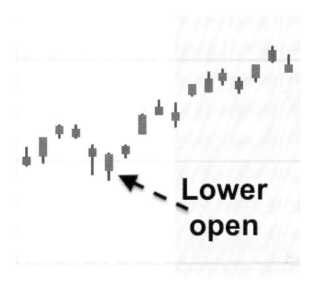

Picture 9

Chapter 3: Follow the Trend

Very often, there are trends in prices in the markets. The trend can be heading up, or it can be heading down. Along the way, our opinion of the trend might be misguided since, in a chaotic system like the stock market, there can be short-term trends that go with or against the overall trend. Recognizing trends and using them to determine the best time to buy is an important skill to develop as a swing trader. In this third chapter, we will introduce some of the concepts associated with trends so that you can start to understand them and understand what to look for when gazing at stock market charts.

Order Flow

Order flow is simply a measure of the number of people buying and selling a given stock at a given time. In other words, are there more buyers or sellers? If there are more buyers, that means the price of the stock is going to be bid upwards, so you might have an upward trend. If there are more sellers, prices are dropping as people are trying to exit the stock, and they are willing to take lower prices to get out since there are not as many people buying, and the buyers want the stock at lower prices.

Later, we are going to talk about using candlesticks, which gives you a graphical representation of order flow. That is a central tool used in technical analysis of stocks and other securities. It allows you to look at the trades that happened in recent time frames and see the order flow in action.

Of course, order flow can be deceptive. You might be in a time period during which more people are selling off stock, but it's about to bottom out, and traders are going to be buying again in the near future. Looking at certain characteristics of charts and candlesticks, you can make estimates of when this is going to happen. However, that always carries inherent risk; things don't always turn out the way they are supposed to behave. Often, the trend starts to reverse for a short time, only to dip back down again.

Trends

There is a saying in the market that the trend is your friend. In reality, this can be a tautology, but at the same time, there is some truth to it. There are times that a share price enters a definite trend. You start to see that on a given stock chart, the trend is moving specifically in one direction or another. Here is a chart for Tesla. It's a five-year chart, and you can see points at which it was advantageous to buy and sell the shares. It can be difficult knowing what appears obvious in retrospect but notice the obvious trends.

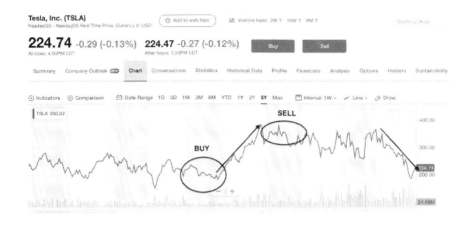

Picture 10

Of course, you can see trends on shorter time scales. A five-year trend is not going to be something that a swing trader is going to be looking at. The point is to get you to start looking for them in stock market charts. Of course, the trick is to get in a given stock at the right time. In a minute, we will talk about support and resistance. Notice the Tesla chart, shown above. Notice that while the stock did go through a high point, it doesn't really seem to drop below a certain level. On the far right of the chart, it looks as though it could be in a position to start trending upwards. To determine that, we'd have to look at a lot of different factors, like recent news about the company and how they are doing as far as meeting manufacturing goals and so on.

Here is a three-month chart of Netflix. Again, right now, we aren't going to worry about the technical details. Instead, use it to start developing an eye for trends.

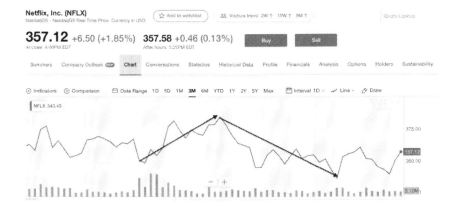

Picture 11

Go to a free site that has stock charts like Yahoo Finance, and start looking at charts for various companies, and also for ETFs that track major indices. Look at the charts over various time frames and start spotting the trends.

Obviously, we are hampered by not having complete information, so it is not going to be possible to be absolutely certain when the price of a stock is entering a trend. Nevertheless, you can put many clues together and estimate when it's good to enter and exit your positions. As always, having preset goals in mind is a good move when making trades. That first trend for Tesla, which was decidedly upward, was a great point to sell and take your profits. As we will see in the next section, there would have been good reasons to do so as a swing trader at that point, but there is no doubt that many people held on, hoping for a renewed rise in price or some big announcement from the company. Instead, since then, the company has continually failed to meet its manufacturing goals, and Elon Musk has engaged in some bizarre behavior, probably causing some investors to pull back. However, despite the problems, Tesla is still a possible long-term bet. Does anyone doubt that in the future more people will be driving electric cars that are doing so at present? If Tesla gets model 3 together and solves their manufacturing and delivery problems, then they are sure to grow market share by a large amount in the future. As a swing trader, it's something to keep your eye on, but you're not going to be interested in whether or not Tesla has a large market share in five years. Your interest is on whether or not within the next 2 days up to six months, Tesla makes a big announcement like a massive increase in manufacturing capability, that will send the share price rising.

Netflix is another animal entirely. It could be primed for more growth in the short term, but it might have entered a period of stagnation. We will see in future chapters how you can investigate these situations to quantify them rather than simply making educated guesses.

Volume

When looking at trends, be sure to follow the volume of trading as well. A high volume coupled with a trend means that the trend is a strong one; many traders are getting in on the action. Low volume can be a signal of indifference. An upward trend with a high volume could be a strong signal that the trend will continue its upward trajectory. However, if the volume is light, that could indicate it's not going to rise much higher.

The Four Phases of Stock Market Trends

Most of the time, the market is following well known but sometimes hard to recognize trends. These are accumulation, expansion, distribution, and contraction. The problem is that it can be difficult to differentiate accumulation from distribution.

During accumulation and distribution, there are long periods during which the price doesn't move very much. The chart may look something like this:

Picture 12

During accumulation, the volume of trading will be relatively low. This indicates that there are few traders or investors who think that the price should be higher or lower or put another way; there is only modest interest in owning the stock or in selling it off. Therefore, the price is relatively stable.

Swing traders should look for an accumulation that lasts several weeks to even months. So how can you tell it from a distribution phase? A distribution pattern will look similar but look for that at the top of an uptrend. Notice that in this chart, there was a steep increase in share price, which we've annotated with the upward pointing arrow. This was followed by a relatively long period (in fact its six months) during which the price stayed at around the same level (circled region) and moved up and down in small increments before plunging.

Picture 13

There can be opportunities for profit during accumulation and distribution. This is trading on the range. However, the opportunities are smaller in magnitude, and you risk getting caught at the start of a major downturn if it's a distribution phase.

The upward trend in the chart is obviously an expansion phase. It could be triggered by any number of things, such as the announcement of earnings that were higher than expected, or the release of a new product. Sometimes, the upward trend will happen over a long time period with some smaller downturns in between the overall upward trend, but in the case shown here, it immediately went into a distribution phase.

In the chart below, we see Tesla in a contraction phase. During contraction, the share price is drifting downward. Notice that there can be upward trends or price rallies throughout the contraction, but the overall trend is clear, the low points are getting lower and lower. At the time of writing, there was a low point of $174 per share that you can see toward the right-hand side, and this has been followed by an increase in share price that has lasted a couple of weeks. It is too soon to tell if this is going to be another rally that ends with a lower low point or not.

Picture 14

Time Scales

Keep in mind that order flow can change over various time scales, and it will have trends that take place on different time scales. As a swing trader, you can choose to operate on a specific time scale or use multiple time scales so you could look for trends over a matter of days. Some swing traders want to get in and out of their trades in a week. Others are willing to hold on for months, waiting for the right opportunity to sell and take profits. Both Tesla and Netflix could be ripe for that approach at the time of writing. The year to date chart for Netflix is pretty interesting – the stock had a steep rise at the beginning of the year, and it's been constant since.

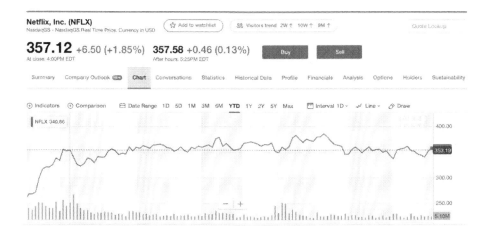

Picture 15

That *could* signal a buying opportunity since Netflix is not
something that's going away anytime soon. Barring any unusual
and unexpected news, there really isn't any reason to expect that
for now. You could expect prices of Netflix to rise in the coming
months. What you will notice about that chart – look at the
horizontal dotted line, is there appears to be a kind of price floor.
We will talk about that more in the next section.

Tesla's year to date charge is a little more dismal. It shows a
steady drop as the months are going by, although there is nothing
catastrophic that's readily apparent.

Picture 16

However, we could be seeing the birth of a new trend. Notice that toward the right side of the chart, the price appears to have bottomed out and it looks like it might be on a slow but steady upward climb. This will require more analysis and digging into the news, to see if there is some substantial reason that investors are taking a more positive view of Tesla. The low price relative to the much higher share price at the beginning of the year indicates there could be a lot of room here for a rise in the share price. It's trading at $224.74 but was at $347 at the beginning of the year. What if it climbed back up to $347? If you bought 1,000 shares now, it would cost $224,740. If it rises to $347, then it would be worth $347,000, and you could sell taking a profit of $122,260. Now keep in mind, that is the only food for thought – you aren't going to enter into swing trades with that kind of magical what if thinking. However, we are looking at the actual stock charts to start to set up what the boundaries are for a given stock and noticed that Tesla *might be* on an uptrend. If it is, that's likely to be the low point of the uptrend, so substantial profits over 3-6 months might be possible. To really get a solid idea about the situation, we would have to do a lot more solid analysis. For now, just use the example to start honing your observational skills when looking at stock market data.

Support

Remember that price floor that we saw with Netflix? This brings us to an important concept called *Support*. Simply put, support is a price floor below which a given stock won't drop below over a specified time period. Or put another way, it's a price point at which buyers tend to start purchasing shares when they see it's a good buy. The pressure of support is enough to keep the price of the stock from dropping further, but it is not strong enough to cause it to break higher – at the moment. However, support is generally seen as a buying opportunity. If you see that a stock is bottoming out at a given support level over your time frame of interest, the support means that the price can either go up or stay at around the support level, making it a good time to buy the shares.

Support represents a bottoming out point below which traders are not willing to sell the stock. It's a point at which there are about as many buyers of the stock as there are sellers. So, support is a level below which the price of the stock is unlikely to decline.

You can quantify this by looking at the amount of noise in the data, and the standard deviation, but many traders simply look for support by reviewing charts. As we will see later, a movement below support or above it can also be indicated by changes in the candlesticks.

In short, a support level is caused by buyers moving into the market to buy shares when the price has dropped low enough to make the purchase appealing. Support happens over a specific time period, so you can determine support by charting a stock over a specific time frame, then drawing a line through the lowest lows of the share price over the time period of interest. Of course, given the chaotic nature of the stock market, that can a slightly idealized description.

In this 5-day chart of SNAP, we see that the support level is about $13.50 a share.

Picture 17

60

Later we will see that there are more sophisticated ways to determine the support level for a given stock, but for now (and even for many practical purposes) this definition will do. The key concept is that the share price seems to struggle to go below the level of support. There is enough interest in the stock that when it drops to the given price level, there are enough people willing to buy shares to keep it from dropping any further. For a time, there may not be enough buyers willing to bid up the price to make it go higher, and so the share price bounces around for a time about the support level. Support means that the share price can break out and start rising. We see that in the SNAP chart (including the sudden massive increase on the right side).

Remember our discussion of stop loss and limit orders? Limit orders can actually create levels of support. So, in the case of SNAP, it could be that many investors have a limit order to buy shares if the share price is around $13.50 a share.

Note that supports don't always hold. Support might break through to the downside meaning that a new, lower support level could form. As we'll see, that is why it is important to keep your eye on multiple indicators. The potential price moves a single indicator might predict don't always hold, and the market sentiment that caused the share price to drop to the support level could get worse, depending on any number of factors. That's why it is important to be up to date on the company, market trends, and financial news. We'll have more to say on support in a moment.

Resistance

You will also see upper boundaries on stock charts that is the price climbs and bounces around a bit at a high level before dropping down again. This is called resistance. That is, the stock price is resistant to going above the given price point. This is a point at which people become resistant to bidding up the stock price any further, and traders are starting to sell to exit their positions.

Looking at a 1-year chart of Amazon, we see a potential level of resistance at about $2040 a share. At least for the time period considered, Amazon doesn't seem able to rise above that price.

Picture 18

Recently it appears to have begun rising, so it will be interesting to see whether or not it is able to break the resistance level and go higher, or whether or not for a third time it edges closer to it and fails to go higher.

How to utilize support and resistance

So now you have an idea of how to spot support and resistance on a stock market chart. So, what does it mean for you as a trader? Stock market pricing over the short term is all about supply and demand. When a lot of sellers enter a market, then supply exceeds demand for the shares and price drops. On the other hand, when demand for a given stock becomes high and lots of buyers enter the market, just like with anything else in economics, the price rises.

Support and resistance are clues to buy and sell opportunities. Let's take resistance first. Moreover, note that for the record we aren't taking shorting a stock as a possibility since that is high risk and advanced strategy that isn't going to be employed by beginners. The goal is always to see a rise in stock price to get profits.

If you have purchased shares, then when you see resistance, that can be a good time to get out. If the price has hit the resistance level, that could be an indication that it's not going to rise any further. Therefore, it would be a reasonable time to sell.

Generally speaking, if a level of support or resistance is breached, that can indicate a major change is coming at the share price so if you see a level of support but then the price drops or starts trending down, that might not be the best time to buy.

Support indicates a good time to buy. As a swing trader, you are always looking to buy low and sell high. If you see support in a stock market chart, that can be a solid indication that the share price is not going to drop any further, and more likely than not it is going to rise again in the near future. That is a strong signal to buy your shares now.

However, we need to take this advice with a grain of salt. No professional trader relies solely on support and resistance lines. They can be taken to be guidelines, rather than true indicators. They can, in many circumstances, be pretty solid. However, you need to consider them with all the other technical indicators that we are going to examine in the book. Then you make your buy and sell decisions based on multiple indicators, giving you more confidence in your decision.

Thinking about how to swing trade

Swing trading is actually quite a simple concept. All you're doing is looking to profit from a swing in price, and the swing doesn't have to be large. You are looking to enter a trade at a reversal and then exit the trade before the opposing pressure takes over. If you are betting on rising prices, you buy at a low point, and then sell at a high point before the bears drive prices back down. You can use recent levels of support and resistance to determine when to enter and exit your trades.

Any move up or down in price is a swing, and they can be used to earn profits. In the example below, the dashed lines represent support (bottom line, the lowest price point for the time period) and resistance (top line, the highest price point that the stock can't break over the time period. The circles are examples of swings. If you are looking to profit from a rise in share price, then you want to buy at the bottom of a swing (at or near the support level) and sell at the top of the swing. If you are interested in shorting the stock, you want to buy at or near the resistance level and sell when the price gets down to the support level, at the bottom of the swing.

Picture 19

Box Patterns

Even if a stock is not about to break out or crash in a downturn, there are opportunities for swing traders to make profits. The first step is to determine the recent levels of support and resistance. These can be used as guidelines in your trades. Your signal for a buying opportunity is when the price drops down back to the support level, and then a reversal starts.

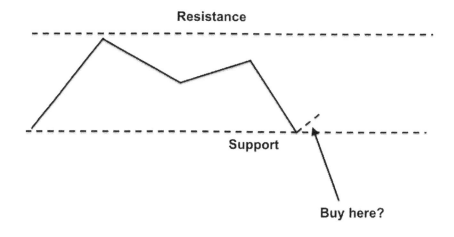

Picture 20

In the example above, the stock price has bottomed out at the support level and is starting to rise. You can buy shares at this point, with a stop-loss order set just below the support level. Your criteria to sell is when the price gets back up to the resistance level.

Of course, there can be risks. Sometimes the support level will be broken, and the price will drop down below it, setting a new lower support level or continually decreasing as we saw with Tesla. You might also see the stock go up a little, then back down to support. You can't know the future so can't be entirely sure that it is going to rise back up to the resistance level, so you will have to use other indicators to determine whether you sell or wait and see if the price zigzags its way back up the resistance level.

Follow the uptrend

During an uptrend, you're still going to see ups and downs most of the time, but generally, the downs are going to be of smaller magnitude than the upswings. You can take advantage of any of the swings to enter into profitable trades. Of course, the earlier you get into a trade, the better.

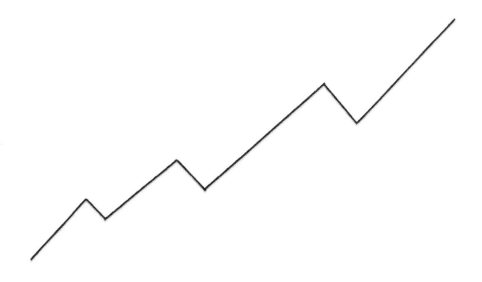

Picture 21

This line chart of Google over several months shows a strong uptrend, and you notice that there are downturns, but for the most part, they are of smaller magnitude than the upturns.

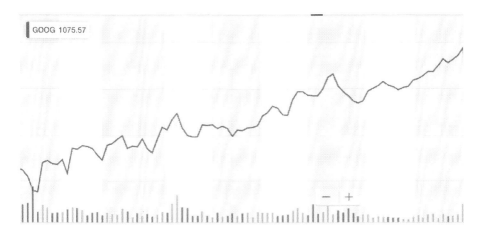

GOOG 1075.57

Picture 22

The small downturns are known as counter trends. You can have counter trends inside the long-term downtrend as well. In that case, the counter trends would be short-term uptrends.

Just as well, you can short a stock and follow the downtrend. In either case, you need to have an exit strategy. Trends don't last for forever, and so you need to plan for an exit assuming that the trend is going to come to a close. If the stock has entered a long-term uptrend, it's hard to know where that is going to be because you're not going to see a level of resistance. However, you have to set a goal for yourself and stick to it; this is best done automatically by placing a limit order so that the shares are sold automatically when the price rises to a certain level.

The example of Google also shows the importance of having stop loss orders. Soon after that uptrend was in full swing, people in Congress started chattering about investigating the tech companies for being monopolies. Google immediately took a tumble.

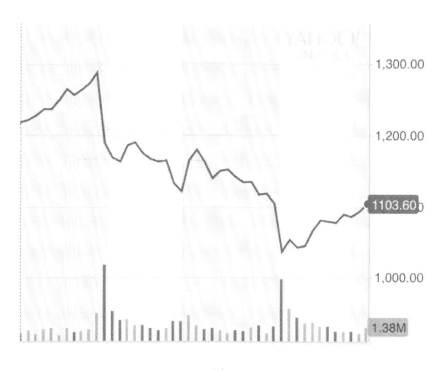

Picture 23

OCO (One order Cancels the other)

One order cancels other order is a way to protect yourself from catastrophic losses, should a trend reversal suddenly catch you off guard. In this case, you place two orders to sell your shares. If one is executed, the other order is canceled.

In the example of Google, a strong uptrend was put to a stop by an unanticipated political event. It's hard to know the exact timing of such events; they can often happen unexpectedly, leading to huge selloffs.

If you set up one order cancels the other order, the first step is to look at the price at which you buy the shares and then set levels of acceptable profits and losses for the trade. As a swing trader, you shouldn't be getting attached to a given stock. You have to accept that sometimes you are going to miss out on further gains, but that is a very small price to pay compared to a crash in stock prices that can leave you in real pain if you haven't protected yourself.

The way you should set this up is to place a stop-loss order that will execute if the price drops to a level that you have defined as the lowest price you can accept when selling the shares. You also place a limit order that you hope will execute if the price rises to a level where you can take solid profits.

As described earlier in the book, you can set your acceptable losses for the trade at 1% or 2% of your total account value. That will offer plenty of protection in any circumstance.

For the limit order to sell at a high price, keep in mind, you don't want to set the price at an unrealistic high that may never be reached. Of course you could cancel the order at any time and sell at a lower price if you have the discipline to do so, but remember that it's easy to get caught up in the idea that share prices are going to keep rising, and so people can fool themselves when seeing a long term upward trend like that. Fear can also play a role here, with fear, in this case, being the fear that you are "missing out" on high profits.

Chapter 4: Technical Analysis

One of the most important toolboxes for the swing trader is technical analysis. You don't have to become as much of an expert at it as a day trader would have to, but it's still very important to understand the basics and pick 2-3 tools to use in analysis to determine what trades to enter, what profit levels to shoot for, and what stop losses you should put in place to protect yourself. Technical analysis can put off a lot of people, but you aren't going to need to do any fancy math, everything is done for you, so all you need is a little bit of understanding of graphs and charts. Most of it is common sense, and you'll be looking for some transitions in your data. With swing trading, the number one error is not looking at the right time frames. You always need to keep your time frame in mind and remember that not all swing traders use the same time frames – so you need to focus on what is appropriate for your personal situation.

Moving Averages

Everyone understands the concept of an average. For the stock market, to get the average price, you simply add up the prices and then divide by the number of points. A moving average means that at each data point, you calculate the average from that data point backward for the number of time steps you want to use. So, if we were using a daily stock chart, a 7-day moving average would calculate the average for the past 7 days at each point, and build up a curve using that data. The reason you want to do this is to smooth out the data into a nice curve, and that is going to give you a better idea of the trend in prices since it weeds out all the noise.

One downside about the moving average is that it's a lagging indicator. That means it's based on past pricing data. Obviously, we can't use a tool that gives us future pricing data. We don't know what that information is. Even so, moving averages give us surprising information that can be useful.

Moving averages used in the stock market analysis are either simple or exponential. What we described above is a simple moving average that is you just add up the number of data points you want and divide by the count.

So, if the price of a stock was $12, $14, $10, $12, and $13 over the past five days, the moving average on the fifth day would be:

MA = $(12+14+10+12+13)/5 = $12.20

If the following day the price is $14.25, the next moving average is:

MA = $(14+10+12+13+14.25)/5 = $12.65

On the stock chart, the value of the MA would be plotted at each point and the values connected into a smooth line. The purple line in this chart shows the 50 days moving average curve for AMD, plotted along with its actual share price.

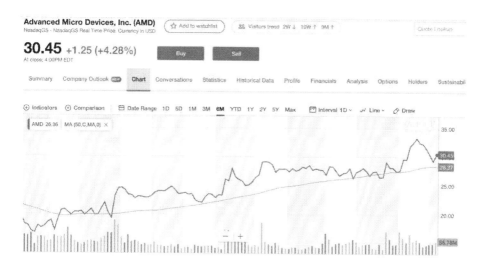

Picture 24

When you add a moving average to a chart, you can select the period and determine whether it uses closing price, open price, high, low, and several other options. Most of the time we will use closing price and the period default (most commonly used value) is 50, which makes the moving average sensitive to prices over the past 50 periods while for a swing trader you'd be interested in days.

Benefits of Moving Averages

In technical analysis, moving averages are going to help you look at two important things. The first is they help identify trends. In a minute we'll see how you can do that. Second, they help you identify support and resistance levels. They do this far better than what you can do by simply drawing straight lines on your charts, even though we spent a lot of time doing that in the last chapter.

Exponential moving averages

You can also generate exponential moving averages. An exponential moving average has a really complicated formula, so we aren't going to work through that part, you can simply use any stock website to add an exponential moving average to a chart. The important thing to remember about exponential moving averages is that they are more sensitive to recent prices. The reason is that the exponential moving average uses weighting that gives more recent prices more emphasis. That makes more sense, especially when you are a swing trader and more interested in shorter-term price changes. With a simple moving average, a price from two months ago has the same weight as yesterday's price, and that might not be relevant to you.

Breaks above and below the long-term MA

Typically, 50-day and 200-day moving averages are used in charts. What you're looking for are movements of the short-term moving average above and below the longer-term moving average. That can indicate a change in trend.

You can see this kind of movement in the chart below, which shows SPY over a one-year period. The purple line is a 50-day simple moving average, and the green line is the 200-day moving average. So, we are looking for points at which the purple line, or shorter-term moving average, crosses above or below the longer-term moving average (the green line).

Picture 25

You can clearly see that the purple line went below the green line before there was a major decline in the share price. So, had you been paying attention, you might have been able to take advantage of the situation either by shorting the stock or perhaps by investing in some put options.

Later, you will also notice that the short-term MA crossed back above the longer-term MA, perhaps indicating an uptrend. The dip you see in the chart is actually a short-term market decline that happened as a result of some tweets from President Trump, so it may not have any real significance related to the longer-term trends.

The data provided by a moving average isn't perfect, but you can use moving averages to estimate support and resistance levels. In an upward trend, a 50-day moving average will give you the support level for the data. So, it can be used to estimate what you should use for your stop-loss price. The position of the current price relative to the 50-day moving average will give you an indication of trend. In our examples, we are looking at past behavior, but you are going to want to look more at current behavior when trying to determine when to enter or exit trades. In the chart for Apple below, notice the position of the handles relative to the purple line, which gives the 50-day moving average.

Picture 26

When the trend is up, the candles are above the 50-day moving average. Then when the trend is down, notice that the candles are below the 50-day moving average. This can help you estimate what the current trend is. You should combine your estimate using this technique with data from other indicators.

Buy signals

When a short term moving average crosses above a longer-term moving average that can be taken as a buy signal if you are hoping for a rising share price. Notice in this chart for Apple, the 10-day moving average has recently crossed above the 50 days moving average, possibly signaling a coming uptrend.

Picture 27

You can also observe from the chart that when the short term moving average crosses below the long-term moving average, you see a sell signal. Indeed, that played out with a declining share price.

Exponential versus Simple Moving Averages

As we said earlier, an exponential moving average is more sensitive to recent prices. Since an exponential moving average is more sensitive to recent prices, it might be able to give us faster insight into coming trend changes. That is, it will detect a trend change before a simple moving average. However, keep in mind that a lot of short-term fluctuations in share price are simply due to noise or random behavior. That means that an exponential moving average might give more weight to meaningless price fluctuations than it should.

In any case, a rising exponential moving average can be taken to indicate a rising share price and vice versa. A good buy signal with the exponential moving average is to look for a rising exponential moving average but with share prices below it. If the exponential moving average is declining, and the stock price dips below it that might mean it's time to sell your shares.

This is noticeable in the chart below, which shows a 50-day exponential moving average. Notice that soon after share prices drop below the moving average, there is a dip in stock prices. This was a solid sell signal in the data, had you been paying attention (or a signal to short). You can also see in this upward trend, the share prices remaining above the exponential average are a solid buy signal.

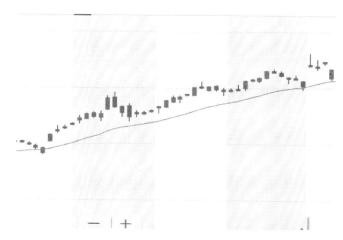

Picture 28

Picture 29

You can also relate exponential moving averages to zones of support and resistance. A downward trending moving average can indicate resistance. If it is upward trending, that can indicate a level of support.

Time Periods

Remember that as a swing trader, you are more interested in longer-term time horizons than a day trader. Maybe you may not be as interested in the type of price weighting that an exponential moving average gives you, but that depends. Swing trading can run from a couple of days out to months. If you are more interested in shorter time frames, then you might prefer looking at exponential moving averages, while if you are interested in months of time for your trades, simple moving averages might work better for you.

Generally speaking, a 20-day moving average can be used to seek out indications of trends. You can also use a 50-day moving average for this purpose. To spot levels of support and resistance, a 100-day moving average is preferred.

Special trading signals

When different period moving averages cross each other, in particular when a shorter period moving average crosses above or below a longer period moving average on the same chart, this can be an important trading signal. A golden cross occurs when a short term moving average crosses above the longer-term moving average. This can be taken as a strong indication of an upward trend in price. When the opposite move occurs, that is a short term moving average crosses below a long-term moving average. This is called a "death cross," meaning that the coming pricing trend is expected to be down.

Bollinger Bands

If you want to identify levels of support and resistance in a stock chart and do it in as close to real time as possible, Bollinger Bands may be the tool that you should be using. Using Bollinger bands, you can find out price levels that stocks are unlikely to break above or fall below in the near future. This can help you figure out exit points (i.e., the selling price you should be willing to accept on trade) and stop-loss orders (the low price you are willing to absorb as a loss).

Bollinger bands are called "bands" because they will show you the two zones of resistance and support simultaneously. You will see the share price fluctuating inside the two bands. This gives us a measure of volatility, but the most important thing about Bollinger bands is that the data they provide is dynamic, that is changing with time. The width of the bands is a measure of the stocks volatility or the magnitude of price swings. Bollinger bands actually include three curves. In the middle, you'll see a moving average.

Since volatility is measured in standard deviations, when you add Bollinger bands, it is going to ask you how many standard deviations you want to use on the chart, along with a period to specify for your moving average. The defaults are 2 standard deviations and a 20-period moving average. Although sometimes you are going to see stock prices go outside the Bollinger bands, for the most part, they stay inside. Here is a chart showing Apple with Bollinger bands over a six-month time period:

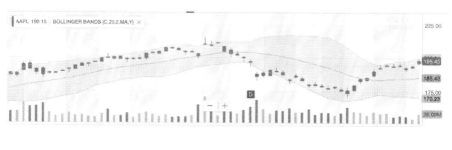

Picture 30

The wider the bands, the more volatility there is in the stock. If the bands are narrow, that indicates low volatility. We will see that Tesla has very little volatility, this is indicated in this chart, and the Bollinger bands are narrow.

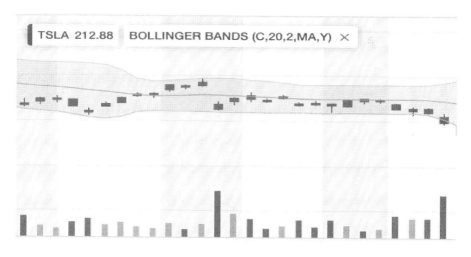

Picture 31

Compare that to the Apple chart, which shows wider Bollinger bands. Apple has much higher volatility than Tesla does.

Bollinger bands also serve other purposes. For example, one thing that traders are interested in is whether or not a given stock is overpriced (at a premium), just right, or low priced (discount). When stock prices are above the moving average, they can be considered to be at a premium that is overpriced. When they drop below the moving average, they are underpriced, so at a discount. They are considered just right when they are at the moving average.

Another thing that traders look at when considering Bollinger bands is whether or not a stock is overbought or oversold. An overbought stock is one set for price declines. To see this in a Bollinger band, look for the wicks of the candlesticks to touch or go outside the upper limit of the Bollinger bands, and expect a price drop thereafter.

An oversold stock can be expected to start trending upward in price. In that case, you want to look for candlestick wicks to touch the lower Bollinger band, or even fall outside of it.

When the body of a candlestick falls completely outside of a Bollinger band, this is taken to be a reversal signal. Two reversal signals are clearly apparent in this chart of SNAP. Two candlesticks whose bodies fell outside the Bollinger bands are noted, and the following trend reversals are apparent.

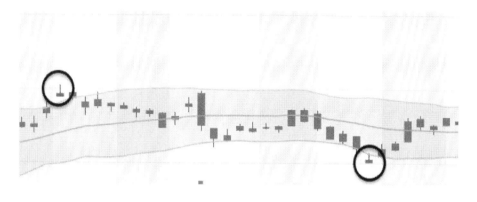

Picture 32

The RSI

The RSI or relative strength index is a measure that sets up boundary values for stock that can indicate overbought or oversold shares. The RSI is a type of oscillator. It can help you determine the momentum a given stock has, giving an estimate of the speed of price movements. If the RSI goes above 70, this is an indication that the stock is overbought. When you see an RSI above 70, that means that a downward trend or price reversal may be coming. If it falls below 30, that indicates the stock is oversold, and an upward trend may be coming.

MACD

MACD means moving average convergence divergence. This fancy title means that you generate an indicator that subtracts the 26-day moving average from the 12-day moving average. That is called the MACD line. A 9-day exponential moving average is also shown, which is the "signal line." If the MACD crosses above the signal line, traders take this as a buy signal. If it does below, that is taken as a sell signal. In the chart below, the orange line is the signal, and the purple line is the MACD line. Notice that the purple line crosses above the signal line, so it's a buy. In fact, on the stock chart above, there was an upward trend after the crossing.

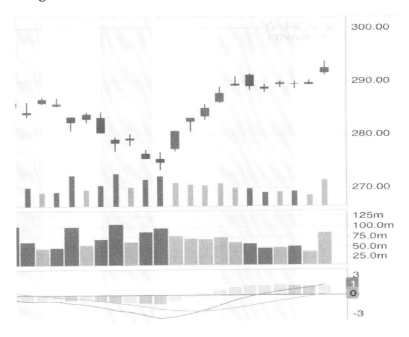

Picture 33

Directional Movement Index

Next, we consider the directional movement index or DMI. This is important because it gives you a measure of the strength of trends, for example, how well did bullish investors do in pushing up the price, or bearish investors do at pushing down the price. These are measured in two trends +DMI and -DMI. The difference between these two trends is called the ADX. On most charts, all three will be shown on the same graph.

Crossovers of +DMI and -DMI are indicators of whether or not bearish investors or bullish investors have stronger momentum. In the chart below, the +DMI line is green, and the −DMI line is red. A point where the +DMI line has crossed below the −DMI line is noted. That would indicate a sell signal, and looking up the dashed line to the stock chart, you see that the share price did decline to a minimum.

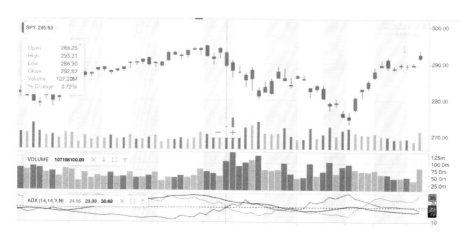

Picture 34

Notice toward the right that there is a point where the +DMI (green line) crossed above the −DMI line (red), indicating that bullish investors had their way. This is born out in the chart where there is a strong upward trend in price after the crossing.

The Hull Moving Average

The Hull moving average was developed to eliminate some of the weaknesses of other moving averages. It seeks to reduce the lagging effect that comes with a moving average more efficiently than an exponential moving average (which used weighting for the same purpose). Typically, a 20 or 50-period Hull moving average is used. It fits stock data to a very accurate degree, and traders look for turns in the curve line to indicate buying and selling signals.

In the chart below, we see a 20-period Hull moving average overlaid on SPY. Notice how nicely it fits the actual pricing data. We have annotated the chart with black arrows that indicate turning points in the curve. When the Hull moving average turns upward, that is an indication of a buy signal. When it turns downward, that is a sell signal. The high accuracy of the Hull moving average is quite impressive, and it seems like a solid indicator to use.

Picture 35

Like other moving averages, you can use short-term, and longer-term Hull moving averages and look for crossover points to get a more accurate indication of a buy or sell signal. The principles used here are the same as those used with other moving averages, so when the short-term Hull moving average crosses above a longer-term Hull moving average, that is a buy signal. On the other hand, when a short-term Hull moving average crosses below a longer-term Hull moving average that can be taken to be a sell signal.

Flags

The next thing we are going to look for is patterns in stock charts that show sudden movement up or down. These are called flags. The analogy here is that the "flagpole" indicates a sharp rise in price over a short time period, while the "flag" can be a zone of stable prices within a narrow range. The chart may look something like this:

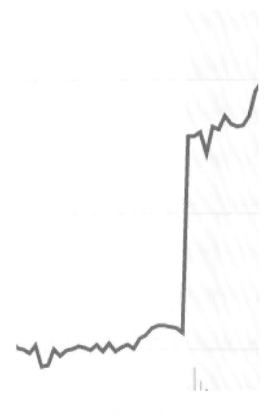

Picture 36

Since the flag, in this case, shot upwards, this is a bull flag. To be a true flag, we need more than just the pattern, you want to check the volume of trading as well. If there is high volume, then the flag can be a signal of further price increases. On the other hand, the price may remain trapped or boxed in at the top of the flagpole, and only fluctuate a bit for a time within the box. In the example above, the stock is SNAP. The volume in the lower area was quite muted, with daily volume ranging between 122k-134k. Entering the bottom of the flagpole, volume shot up to 719k. At the top of the flag pole, it shot up again, to 1.6 M. The large increases in volume are indicative that this is a solid opportunity and a real bull flag. In fact, carrying it out a few days later, we see more increases in share price:

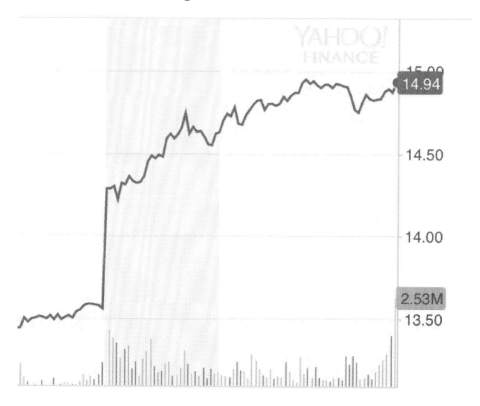

Picture 37

As you can see from the bars at the bottom of the chart, the volume remains strong all the way to the right-hand side. Entering a trade at the top of the flagpole would have been a reasonable move for a swing trader. To have a successful trade, you can put a stop loss order of 1% risk below the top of the flag pole. You have to be prepared for the situation where the top of the flag is going to be a resistance, rather than a true breakout. In this case, it's a true rise in the share price. Always pay attention to volume.

Of course, flag patterns can be inverted and work for suddenly declining prices as well. In that case, it's a bear flag. Again, knowing whether or not it's a true flag can hinge on volume. Always compare the volume to see if traders are flocking to the stock or selling it off. Low volume indicates that there isn't much interest in the stock as far as buying and selling right now, and so the price move may not be significant and you might be witnessing a move to support or resistance instead.

So, if a flag is real, where does this come from? More than likely, it comes from a significant announcement by the company or a surprising earnings call. That is, the company may have had an earnings report that beat expectations. We discuss these items in the chapter on fundamentals, and if you are a good trader, you are paying attention to fundamentals and not just technical indicators. That means that you would know this might be coming or be ready to act on it before anyone else (anyone else, among individual investors), instead of staring at charts looking for mysterious patterns. Of course, we aren't saying to use the technical analysis or look for patterns like this in the charts – but rather that you should do both and sometimes take your nose out of the trees. That means paying attention to financial and business news and reading about the companies you are interested in trading.

How many indicators can you use?
There are many indicators – maybe even too many. Looking at all of them will make your head spin. Are you supposed to use all of them?

In fact, we haven't even covered all of them. I invite the reader to open up a stock chart on Yahoo Finance or their favorite trading website and explore all the possible indicators they can add onto their charts.

The reality is at some point, you are not going to be getting any additional information from paying attention to more and more indicators. You are going to have to settle on a small number of indicators and accept the results that come from that.

First off, every trader should use basic chart reading. That is a common sense level of analysis, but it is still important. It's the starting point of any analysis but shouldn't be your final guide to making a decision to enter a trade or not.

Second, candlesticks are time tested and proven method. But remember that candlesticks are not fool proof, they only serve as a guide. But it's a solid guide to include in your analysis. It's hard to find a trader – any trader – who is not using candlesticks. You should take your time to study them well beyond the introductory information that we've provided in this book.

So, we are at a point where you should use candlesticks and eyeball charts for levels of support and resistance. What about all the others? Certainly, using moving averages is useful, but you shouldn't get caught up in picking which moving averages to use. They all have merits and drawbacks. I have found the Hull moving average to be pretty exceptional.

Bollinger bands are also useful, especially as an aid in determining the levels of support and resistance.

The bottom line is that adding more and more indicators is not going to give you more information in the end. Many of the different indicators are different flavors of the same information. So, settling on one of the other might even be said to come down to a matter of personal taste.

It's also better to thoroughly understand and use 1-2 indicators than it is to have a shallow use of 10 different indicators. Our personal preference is to use candlesticks, Bollinger bands, and Hull moving averages, and we don't even always use Bollinger bands. But we are not here to tell you which ones to use, you can use this book as a guide for introducing you to the world of indicators, and then study them in detail elsewhere and make the choices that fit you the best. You might also end up changing things as time moves on, trying different indicators, and finding out that others work better for you.

Remember that there is no magic tool that is going to guarantee riches. The indicators are there to help you make your trades, but they cannot tell you what trades to make. In the end, the best indicator is the one between your ears, and you will have to be the one that does the analysis and makes the decisions. Not all decisions are going to be the right ones, and even experienced traders make bad trades, so when it gets down to it don't blame the indicators, some trades are just not going to work out.

Chapter 5: Company Fundamentals

When swing trading, all the focus seems to be on all these indicators that can show us where the market is going to go. Nevertheless, one thing you need to keep in the back of your mind is that you are not a day trader, and you should even be willing to go for a long time period (relatively speaking) on your trades. That might be several months, but always less than a year. However, unlike day traders, one thing we need to keep in mind is that the company fundamentals are important for swing traders to study as well. Keeping up with the details of company operation will help you be well placed to profit from swing trades timed with earnings calls or the release of a new product.

Financial statements

In order to properly assess the value of a company's stock, you are going to need to have a solid handle on the finances of the company. That doesn't mean you need to become an accountant, but before entering a large trade on a company's stock, you should have a look at all of their financial statements. It turns out that swing trading is going to overlap with the type of analysis someone like Warren Buffett would do when buying a stock. Knowing whether a stock's current price is over- or under-valued is an important starting point before making bets on future swings in the price.

In order to get enough information to make informed swing trades, you don't have to go to a great extent in reviewing this information. Most of this information is available on sites like Yahoo Finance. The information you need is going to be under a tab labeled *Financials* after you select a particular stock. There, you will find three things to look at – the income statement, balance sheet, and cash flow.

Yahoo Finance lets you view the information on an annual basis or quarterly. First, let us familiarize ourselves with what we can find inside each report.

Income Statement

The income statement can give you a plethora of information about the health of the company. This is going to include revenue, gross profit, operating expenses, income from continuing operations, and net income. One thing you'll want to keep your eye on when viewing the income statement is to look at the annual values and see how they are changing with time. Did the company experience growth over the past five years? Is the growth continuous or is this a company in decline?

Cash Flow

Next, you can look at the cash flow for the company. Cash flow includes net income, operating activities, investing and financing activities, and changes in cash or cash equivalents. One thing to look for is companies that are borrowing a lot, which may not be a sign of good health. Of course, you should always look at the amount borrowed relative to the earnings, just as you would for an individual. Companies that have lower levels of long-term debt (33% or less relative to equity) are healthier investments than companies that are saddled with a lot of long-term debt relative to equity.

Balance Sheet

Finally, let's introduce the balance sheet, which shows you the current assets and liabilities, as well as the stockholder's equity in the company. Look for companies that have a lot of cash on hand and not so much debt (Apple is a great example).

Of course, you can get a great deal of information about a company that isn't available from these sights, but the U.S. Securities and Exchange Commission requires companies to provide a wide range of information. You will want to read through the prospectus of any company that you are entering into a large trade with. In addition, there are some SEC required reports that can be of interest.

SEC-Required Filings

The first SEC report that is of interest to investors is the 10K. Here you will not only find the companies audited financial statements, but you will find information about the management team, what markets the company is doing business in, information about the company's competitors, and information about its history. A 10Q will include quarterly financial statements. Some companies must also file an 8K, which is a report filed when there is a special event that the company must bring to the attention of shareholders.

Earnings Reports

One of the events in a company's annual life that is of utter importance to swing traders are earnings announcements and calls. These happen on a quarterly basis but will be on different dates for different companies. These events represent big investment opportunities for swing traders. In particular, you are going to be looking for companies that beat the expectations of the market. When this happens, the big price upswings can be expected to follow. Meeting expectations is also good, but failing to meet expectations can lead to price declines, even if the company was profitable. Either way, these all represent opportunities for the swing trader. If a company fails to meet expectations or even loses money, you can short the stock and still make profits.

Past quarterly reports can give you insight into how things might go in the next earnings call. You should be studying those as well as reading up on what analysts are expecting for the company this time around.

Bad Signs

The following are bad clues for the company's future:

- Large levels of debt. If the company has long-term debt that is 33% or more of the total amount of equity, that is a bad sign.
- Sudden increases in inventory: If the inventory is increasing rapidly, it may mean that the company is entering a period where sales are slowing. That means a bad earnings report.
- High levels of current liabilities. You don't want a company that can't manage its debt.
- Sudden increases in accounts receivable. That might mean the company has clients that aren't paying their bills.
- High levels of short-term debt.
- An increasing ratio of current liabilities to current assets. Compare quarter to quarter to see if there is a trend. A company taking on more debt as time goes on is a bad investment.

Example: Tesla

Let's take a look at the financial statements of a couple of companies. First, we'll look at Tesla, which seems to be constantly mired in problems despite the promise of the company. Looking at their current liabilities, total current liabilities have increased from $2.85 billion at the end of 2015 to $9.9 billion by the end of 2018. That is a red flag to consider. However, looking at the past four quarters, there has been some improvement in current liabilities, with it dropping to $9.24 billion in the last quarterly report. Long-term debt was $9.65 billion in the last quarterly report. Total shareholder equity was $4.6 billion, so long term debt is more than twice as large! Do you want to invest in a company with those kinds of financials? The answer is that it depends, but those are not good signs. You'll have to keep an eye on earnings reports and whether or not they get their act together in being able to manufacture and deliver cars.

Another bad sign- inventory jumped 23% in the last quarterly report relative to the previous one. That could indicate a sales slowdown. In fact, looking at the last quarterly report net income actually was in the negative, a substantial drop from the previous quarter.

Unless there is something that is going to turn the company around fast, right now this is not a good investment.

Example: Apple

Apple is constantly getting beat up in the news because increases in their sales are not as big as they used to be. However, if you look at all the fundamentals, Apple looks quite healthy. First, note that, on an annual basis, after a substantial drop in net income in

2016, it's risen and in 2018 was higher than 4 years earlier, when Apple was still considered the dream company. Long-term debt was $93.7 billion at the end of 2018, but total stockholder equity was $107 billion. Better than Tesla, but at 88%, still a lot higher than we'd like to see it. Inventory went up in the last quarter of 2018 but has dropped since, so that is a hopeful sign, at least they are moving some product despite the constant haranguing by the media. In addition, if you look at the quarterly reports for Apple rather than annual, you'd see that current liabilities have dropped substantially. On 9/29/2018, they stood at $117 billion, but that figure had dropped to $93.7 billion in the latest report. Long-term debt also dropped by $3.5 billion from 9/29/18 to the last quarterly report and it's down from $97 billion for the quarter ending 6/30/18. Apple looks to be doing better than Tesla and getting itself into a more secure position. When looking at Apple, since their revenue is often cyclical depending on release dates for important products, you should compare annual values or year-over-year values for the same quarter. On an annual basis after two years of declines, in 2018 they showed solid numbers that were much higher than four years earlier. Apple also has a substantial R&D budget, indicating they are continuing to develop new products for future growth. Tesla's R&D budget is surprisingly puny in comparison.

Examining Earnings

When looking at earnings, you'll want to see how gross profit changes as a percentage of revenue and operating income as a percentage of revenue. Tesla's gross profit as a percentage of total revenue has remained fairly consistent at around 18% or so, but they have had several years of negative operating income. However, it has shown dramatic improvement over the past two years.

Apple's gross profit has also been fairly consistent as a fraction of total revenue, but it's about a stunning 44%. Operating income is positive and increased from just under 7% to 7.4% going from 2017 to 2018. Again, Apple looks to be in better shape than Tesla.

Relative Valuation

When using fundamental analysis swing traders should focus on relative valuation. This compares the value of a company to competitors in the same industry. That can help you determine where the company's share price sits relative to similar companies in the same industry. A low-priced share relative to other companies in the same industry for a valuable company can represent a buying opportunity. A simple way to do this is to look at the price to earnings ratio, not by itself but by comparing it to other companies in the same industry. For Apple, the most recent price to earnings ratio is 26.44. Google, which makes the Android operating system, is probably about as close a competitor as we can come up with, if the price to earnings ratio is 27.69. Smartphone competitor Samsung doesn't trade on U.S. exchanges, so a comparison isn't possible.

With Tesla, it's hard to say if comparing them to other automotive companies is a fair comparison, since they've occupied a unique niche by selling only electric vehicles. Nevertheless, we could look at automotive companies amongst themselves to see if there are any suggestive data in the PE ratio. Ford checks in at 13, General Motors at 5.84, Toyota at 7.67, and Honda at 4.47. This would require a lot more analysis, but it is interesting that Ford is such an outlier. The low values for the other companies could indicate they are good buys, but you have to look at all the other data to determine this. For example, you would want to look at the net profit margin and other metrics to see how Ford compares with the competition. It may be that Ford is in better shape and deserves a premium share price, or it may be significantly overvalued, indicating there could be an opportunity to short the stock.

Price Multiple as a Trading Goal

If you find a company that appears to be undervalued, this can be a candidate for a swing trade. Keep in mind that this isn't necessarily an opportunity for overnight profit; you might have to stay in this trade over weeks or months. Nevertheless, it's an interesting strategy.

After doing a complete analysis of the financial data for representative companies in an industry, pick the company you want to use for a swing trade. You are going to want to evaluate where the share price for the company stands relative to the industry as a whole using the P/E ratio – premium, discount, or where it should be. If the P/E ratio is at a discount, then you can buy shares of the stock anticipating rising share prices in the coming months, perhaps after the next earnings call. You could also short a stock trading at a premium. In the case of the automotive industry, Ford's outlier status doesn't appear to be justified, so it might be a candidate for a short. In fact, Ford and GM both show declining profits and Fords Gross profit as a share of revenue is about the same as GM's – indicating its P/E ratio is high, so Ford is priced at a premium relative to others in the same industry. A more in-depth analysis would be required before actually entering into a trade, but that is certainly a strong indicator that the share price is too high.

Systemic vs. Unsystematic Risk

There is a risk to the market as a whole, which is related to the condition of the overall economy. This is called *systemic* risk. *Unsystematic* risk is a risk related to a particular stock. If a stock doesn't add any risk to your portfolio, then it only has systemic risk. If the stock is in danger of crashing, because of bad news or a scandal, but the rest of the economy is fine, it carries a lot of unsystematic risks. These concepts are important when considering the volatility of an individual stock.

Volatility

One of the characteristics of a stock that a trader needs to be familiar with is volatility. Simply put, it is the range of prices over which stock will vary for a given time frame taken together with the number of times it fluctuates. So colloquially, a stock with a lot of volatility is going to be one that moves up and down a lot over short time periods. The chart will have a lot of zigs and zags, while a stock with low volatility will have a smoother appearance and not nearly as much movement. In short, volatility gives you a measure of how much the price of a stock has moved in the past and how rapidly it has done so. High volatility in the past might indicate high volatility in the future but remember that is not a guarantee of high volatility going forward.

Swing traders might be more interested in stocks with high volatility because that means there are going to be more opportunities to take profits, and if the stock is really volatile the larger swings in price could indicate that there are also opportunities for higher profits. The volatility of a stock is measured by calculating its standard deviation, but most readers probably aren't interested in the details. You can get a measure of the volatility of the stock by looking at *Beta*, which is available from any service or website that gives information about stocks.

High levels of volatility raise the risk associated with the investment, but also raise the potential for profitable returns.

Beta tells you how volatile a given stock is relative to the market as a whole. The market is taken to have a Beta of 1.0. If the Beta for a given stock is greater than 1.0, it's a volatile stock. If Beta is less than 1.0, it's a stock with the volatility that correlates to the market as a whole.

If Beta is 1.0, then the stock carries only systemic risk. It doesn't add to the risk of the market, the only risk the stock has is the systemic risk of the market as a whole (collapse as in great depression or dot com crash). The lower that Beta is, the less volatility the stock has, and so the less risk, generally speaking. However, this also means that the probability that the stock will provide high returns at least in the near future is lower.

If a stock has a beta of 1.4, then its 40% more volatile than the market as a whole. If there are strong, indicators that the price of the stock is going to increase in the near term that might make the stock a good buy for the swing trader.

A stock with a beta at 0.80 is less volatile than the market as a whole. It's 20% less volatile to be precise, and this can be thought of as a bit of a boring investment.

Beta can be positive or negative. If it's negative, that means that the volatility of the stock goes against the market.

Beta (3Y Monthly):

- Amazon 1.73: That means that Amazon has been 73% more volatile than the market as a whole.
- Apple 1.03: Apple is right with the stock market, so only carries systemic risk.
- Tesla 0.03: That is an odd one, Tesla has no volatility. However, if you look at its chart for the past three years, you'll see that from February 2017 through March 2019, the price was relatively constant, fluctuating around the same price points.
- Netflix: 1.51: It's 51% more volatile than the market.
- NRG: 0.53: This is a utility stock. They are notorious for having low betas, and this indicates the stock is pretty stable.

Keep in mind that low volatility doesn't mean the stock price isn't going up or down with a long-term trend, it just means that it is not doing it with wild swings up and down over shorter time periods.

Read the Prospectus

You need to have an idea of where a company is going. Remember, stock trading is about the future, not the past. We can get caught up in looking at the charts and indicators, along with financial statements. All of that is important for sure, but so is where the company is headed. For example, if you are willing to invest in a pharmaceutical company, then you might want to have knowledge about what drugs, if any, it has under development. If one is about to get FDA approval that could be a game changer for the stock price. You will also be interested in things like their R&D budget. Companies spending on R&D have an eye toward the future, and better prospects going ahead. Now of course as a swing trader you aren't interested in a 10-15 year time horizon – but you are looking for any characteristics that make a solid company that can be worth betting on over the short term and the long term.

Chapter 6: Trading Index Funds

Most swing traders think in terms of trading shares of individual companies, but you can swing trade shares in exchange-traded funds and make great profits as well. One of the most popular ETFs is SPY, which is invested in the S & P 500, a pretty good metric for the entire market. It may surprise some readers to learn that SPY is one of the most popular trades when it comes to options. It's worth looking into for swing trading as well.

Different risks

The S & P 500 has a heavier weight of systemic risk as compared to the stock for an individual company. That might be obvious, but it's important to get that out upfront. When some news items come out with an impact on the entire market, SPY is likely to see huge gains or possibly huge losses while individual stocks like Apple or AMD might not feel any impact. Therefore, if you are going to trade SPY, one thing you're going to want to do is keeping a close eye on the news.

Most index funds are going to face the same issue so you're going to want to be looking at things like changes in interest rates, and even an offhand remark by the chairman of the Fed can send investors into a panic. Trade deals or remarks and tweets by the President can also send markets tumbling, or going upward.

Good jobs reports and GDP growth reports can send them skyrocketing.

Generally, the market as a whole sees routine increases over longer periods as a result of economic growth but, of course, you'll need to have some consciousness about recessions and the inevitable economic downturns.

A lot of that goes on hunches, but you can also look at the P/E ratios of different market segments. These include the S & P 500, mid-cap companies, small-cap companies, and the market as a whole. It turns out that Standard and Poors maintains this information, and you can make comparisons of historical values to today's P/E ratios to determine whether prices are inflated.

You can view a graph of the data and look up some past values here:

Category: Market Indices and Statistics

Region: United States

Report: S&P 500 Earnings

Source: Standard and Poor's

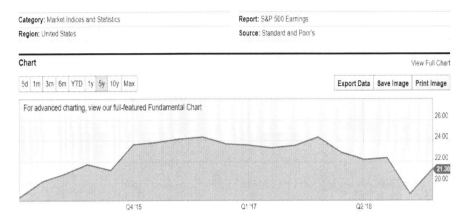

https://ycharts.com/indicators/sp_500_pe_ratio

Opportunitics

Looking at SPY just over the past year, we can see that there were many opportunities to profit from swing trades. Just recently, the price dropped to $274 per share. Two weeks later, it had risen to nearly $293 a share, quite a substantial increase. On 12/24/18, it was $239 a share, about a month later it was $266 a share.

Those are pretty substantial price moves, and many stocks don't have moves that large. Therefore, it's something to consider adding to your trading mix.

The many options available

There are exchange-traded funds for everything under the sun, and the important thing to remember as a swing trader is that although the underlying assets for the funds may not be stocks, the funds themselves trade like stocks. This opens up all kinds of investment opportunities. For example, you can swing trade precious metals. The exchange-traded fund GLD tracks the price of gold, and just glancing at the chart over the past year, several swing trading opportunities should jump out at you.

Picture 39

The same holds true for SLV, the iShares silver trust. Silver may not be a good investment, but as a swing trader, you can profit from its price moves:

Picture 40

You can also use exchange-traded funds to swing trade other financial assets through the stock market. This includes Forex trading, so you can buy and sell shares of stock and indirectly do Forex trading. FXE is a fund that backs the Euro against the dollar. It also shows many opportunities for swing trades:

Picture 41

Alternatively, you could track the dollar:

Picture 42

These currency charts are three-month charts, and you can see both have multiple entry and exit points that could have been used for good swing trades. Of course, making good judgments about these trades means that you have to study the Forex market and keep up with economic news.

Other opportunities exist, including swing trading some investments that aren't normally available to swing trade. Another interesting possibility is using exchange-traded funds to swing trade bonds.

The point here isn't to promote trading any specific fund or asset class, but rather to open your eyes to the potential. You aren't limited to just trading individual stocks but remember: no matter what you invest in, you should use the same principles, which means doing your homework, watching trends closely, and following your indicators.

Chapter 7: The Swing Trader Mindset

Becoming a swing trader isn't for everyone. In chapter Seven, we are going to discuss some of the mistakes you might make at the beginning, as well as the proper swing trader mindset.

All of us were inexperienced beginners at one time. Beginners are prone to making mistakes in any endeavor. The problem with the stock market is making mistakes can be extremely costly when you are a trader, even leading to bankruptcy. Nevertheless, by learning from the mistakes of others, you can avoid falling prey to the biggest problems that might come your way as a result of your inexperience.

Failing to exit a losing trade

It can't be said enough; all too often people let emotions take over their judgment in the stock market. When you set up a big swing trade, you might get overconfident and excessively excited about it if you are new to the business. Moreover, if the stock starts moving the wrong way, you might hold onto the trade when you should simply exit and take your losses. Sometimes people can't believe it when a "sure thing" turns out to be a loss, and they hold on too long hoping things are going to turn around. Waiting too long can be costly —sometimes catastrophically so. We hate to beat a dead horse – but protect every trade you make with stop-loss orders rather than letting emotion take over.

Exiting Too Soon

The right time to exit a trade can be a difficult thing to figure out. That's why it's best to plan ahead of time and set an exit point where you are going to be comfortable with profits. If you go into a swing trade without a definite plan, it's going to be too easy to fall prey to a situation where you might get out too soon, afraid that you aren't going to be able to make any profit and fearing possible losses. You can also get fooled by temporary downturns. Remember that there are always counter trends on the way up. Don't be fooled by the counter trends into exiting too early. Emotion can get heavy immediately after placing a big trade. Also, remember that you should set a time frame for your trade to work out. Swing traders are not day traders, so don't get the impulse to exit a trade two hours after you've entered the position.

Believing shares won't lose value

Unbelievably, some people have the same attitude about stocks that people used to have about housing, which is that stocks won't decline. Sometimes they do, and they don't recover. Just because it's Google or Apple, it doesn't mean that losses aren't possible.

Too much margin

Swing traders can actually access a lot of margins. That means that you can borrow to buy shares from the broker. That can be a problem if you end up losing big, you might end up owing the broker a large amount of money. You need to be extremely careful with margin, and all things considered, it is better to grow slowly by making methodical trades with money you already have than it is to borrow lots of money in hope of quickly growing your account.

Waiting too long for price declines

There are ideal price points to buy shares. However, you shouldn't always wait to reach a level of support before buying. Sometimes a stock might be entering an upward trend, and it's going to establish a new level of support. If you wait too long hoping the price is going to drop down to the last level of support, you might miss out on the opportunity.

Believing past performance is a guarantee of future performance

This is one of the biggest fallacies of the stock market. You cannot take the past performance of a company's stock as an ironclad guarantee that the stock is going to perform the same way going forward. Past performance indicates little compared to the company's current fundamentals, trading volume, volatility, and the trends and indicators for the stock in the here and now. Just because Amazon grew a lot in the past five years, it doesn't mean it will continue to do so.

Investing more than you can afford to lose

It's easy to get excited about the amount of money you can make swing trading, and it's also easy to get excited over all the charts, all the action, and the thrills of making winning trades. This can lead some people into pulling out too much money from savings and retirement accounts to enter into larger trades. That is a big mistake. You should always keep in mind that you need to set up trades where you can afford to lose it all, so your personal savings, college savings accounts, and retirement accounts won't be impacted, and you won't have trouble paying for your basic living expenses. Set aside the excitement and prepare for a long journey where you grow your business slowly, so you don't end up in the poor house.

Get started with small and achievable profit goals, and when your trades go bad as some inevitably will, your losses will be minimal.

Now we'll look at the swing trader mindset. This will be a mix of characteristics and attitudes you should have before even becoming a swing trader, and also a set of behaviors and mindsets you should adopt once you become a swing trader.

You must be Risk Tolerant

Most investors have a low tolerance for risk. That is why they put money in savings accounts and mutual funds. Becoming a swing trader can be said to put you in an elite community. That isn't to say that swing traders are better people. What we mean by this is that swing trader are a small group relative to the overall population. The vast majority of people are not willing to risk their capital in order to realize large, short-term gains. While a swing trader is more cautious (and some would say more rational) than a day trader, compared to the average outlook that most people have if you are interested in swing trading that indicates a much higher tolerance of risk.

You are not ruled by emotion

A successful swing trader is not going to be someone who is ruled by emotion. You are going to enter into and exit your trades based on a cold, hard examination of the facts. Someone who is caught up in emotion when stocks start moving up fast or sliding down is not someone who is suitable to be a swing trader. Emotional decisions can lead to many bad trades and can even be catastrophic. The average person can panic when a certain trend appears in the stock market. There is no room for panic if you decide to become a trader, keeping a cool head at all times is essential.

You do your homework

A swing trader is not going to trade based on their gut. That is something amateurs do. Of course, we always hear the winning stories, but most of the time people trading on their gut are going to lose out. As a successful swing trader, you should be trading based on a thorough background check of the situation. You should be doing your homework by picking 2-3 of your favorite technical analysis tools, studying candlesticks and trends, and also studying the fundamentals of the company and keeping up with financial news. Only after you've thoroughly evaluated a stock should you consider entering into a trade. People who don't do their homework might win some of the time, but at the end of a year when you compile all the wins and losses, people that don't do their homework are going to finish last unless they got very lucky. The world isn't governed by luck unless you're at a gambling casino. Despite the unfair reputation, trading might have among the ignorant public, swing trading is not gambling, and so isn't governed by luck.

You are disciplined

A swing trader is disciplined. This really follows on the heels of the previous point, but a swing trader is someone that studies everything carefully and takes the time to study all of the technical analysis indicators and trends they are going to use in their analysis. Then you will have the discipline to develop a trading plan, and you're going to have the discipline to stick to the trading plan. When becoming a swing trader, whether you're going to do it full-time or only on a part-time basis keeping your day job, you need to look at swing trading as a business. You wouldn't run a business based on temporary emotional outbursts. If you did, you could easily end up broke. For example, suppose you find some kind of craft made in China and open a shop to sell them. The third day your shop is open; someone comes in and praises them and buys three. You get super excited. Do you then take your entire life savings and buy 1,000 more? We hope not.

Swing trading needs to be approached in the same way. View it as a business and make a business plan that you are going to follow. You are not going to get rattled by missing out on potential gains in the share price. For one thing, until any gains happen, they are nothing but imaginary. It is better to sell when you can do so and take a profit. Second, you are not in this to make a large profit off one trade. Of course, if you have a great trade, all the more power to you. However, generally speaking, swing trading is about earning money steadily from trades over the long term and slowly growing your business. It is not a get rich quick scheme, so don't think of it that way. If you can make a $1,000 profit from a trade, you are doing quite well, and you can reinvest the money to continue to grow your business with time. Any time you are making profits from a trade, it is going to be a time to be happy, even if it is only $100.

Amateurs are the ones who are going to fret because they "missed out." More often than not, share prices are going to drop off from some peak if you hold on too long, and you will miss out on what you could have had if only you had the discipline to sell at the right time. That is more dangerous than missing out on some "big thing" that could have netted you huge returns.

You prepare for all outcomes

As part of running your swing trading as a business, a good swing trader prepares for all outcomes. That is why we included the one order cancels another approach in this book. Everyone expects profits, but they don't always materialize. Therefore, you need to be as prepared for losses - in fact, more so – as well as being prepared to cash in profits. Preparing for all outcomes means first determining the risk level you are willing to accept for your account. You have to set a risk level you are comfortable with, the 1-2% level is recommended by market experts, but that doesn't mean you have to follow it exactly. However, no matter what you do need to set a level of risk so that if you did lose the capital, you are not going to be hurt financially. Of course, any loss of capital hurts, but you shouldn't be having to go into debt or begging on the street corner to make your house payment because you made a bad trade. You also need to make sure that not only are your losses not catastrophic, but if you do take a loss, you still have enough money to enter into another trade.

Also, be aware of creeping losses. If you keep losing $500 per trade without making any gains, you need to take a look at your trading practices and dial back your level of risk. A $500 loss one time is one thing, a $500 loss every week can add up fast.

You can adjust your strategy

Emotion can take over in many ways when trading. Money has that effect on people. One way that emotion can overtake you is if you develop your own system for swing trading, and you start making multiple winning trades. Then something in the market might change, and maybe you start losing lots of money. In that case, are you going to be beholden to your old system, or adjust to the changing conditions? A successful trader is going to be one who makes the adjustments. Don't take it personally, when things stop working. Always fall back on doing the analysis, remember that hard facts rule the day at all times, not your love of Apple, Netflix, or even your own trading methods.

You might also take a look at what indicators you are using. Maybe it's time to try different indicators. On the other hand, maybe you are even relying on indicators too much, or putting too much stock in trends.

Successful traders don't stop learning

This book should be taken as your first step. A successful trader is one who is open to continuous education. There are always things to learn from others that can help make you a better trader. You should be putting in an effort to educate yourself to grow your knowledge about finance, the stock market, and business. That includes watching YouTube videos, taking courses, and reading as many books about the subject as you can. You should also watch plenty of financial news so you can learn about current conditions and how people think they are going to change. They aren't always going to be right, but the more knowledge you have, the better positioned you are going to be when it comes to being a successful trader.

Don't give in to euphoria or despair

We are all going to have big winning trades and massive losses at one point or another if we trade for any length of time. Whether you experience a big loss or not is not the question, it's how you react to it. Persistence and objective analysis about what went wrong with the trade are the proper ways to respond. Falling into emotional despair is unproductive and doesn't help the situation. First off, if you give in to emotional despair, you are not going to learn from your mistakes. You are also letting your emotions take over and take control of your actions. Of course, if you have followed the principles outlined in this book, you won't have any catastrophic losses – but if you do then review the principles behind managing risk, dust yourself off and try again.

Euphoria over a big winning trade can be as damaging. Book your winning trades and be happy about them, but don't let yourself be overcome by mania. Also, don't waste money. Sure, you can take a little out to celebrate, but again, you should treat this as a business and reinvest most of your profits. Long-term growth of your business should be the number one goal. If you are living off your trades, only take out what you need to take out. Don't blow a winning trade on a new car and a trip to Europe. It's also important because it might lead you into entering into a lot of bad trades in the aftermath. Sometimes people can get overconfident and then blow themselves out of the water because they let their euphoria take over and they overtraded.

Chapter 8: Finding a Broker

Some people reading this book may not have managed their own stock trading before. If it's your first foray into having an individually managed account, that can be intimidating, and you may not know where to begin. There are a few issues to consider and many choices available. Let's explore some of these briefly here.

Commissions

These days one of the biggest issues to consider when choosing a brokerage is whether they charge commissions, and if so, how big are they? Just a few years ago, this was not even a question that anyone would even bother asking, but today there are several brokerages that don't charge any commissions at all. As a swing trader who frequently trades compared to your standard buy-and-hold investor, you might find that commissions can eat into your profits. Luckily, commissions are either dropping or even zero at many brokerages. The presence of zero-commission brokerages is also putting pressure on the old school brokers who have been used to charging high commissions and fees. Downward pressure on prices is a signal that market competition is good.

One bit of advice is that you'll want to consider new brokerages. First, they tend to have zero commissions. Older stockbrokers like Charles Schwab are going to charge higher commissions as a rule. Do your research before making a decision.

Resources

One thing you might consider is how much the broker devotes to providing resources that you can utilize to do your research without having to go somewhere else. Unfortunately, some of the no commission brokers fall short in this department. That may or may not be important since there are tons of free resources available on the internet. One of the best is Yahoo Finance, which has been around for more than two decades. It is very helpful with financial statements and nice interactive charts that let you use many of the tools we have been discussing in the book (and showing in many of the charts). It's all free, so there really isn't a need to have a broker provide that for you, but it's something to consider.

Venue

Do you want an online broker? What about one with an app, or both? These days the old school way of doing things, going to an office where you actually meet a stockbroker, is something that has been replaced by electronic tools and that makes perfect sense given the way the markets work. Recently many brokers have been expanding past the traditional internet to offer apps as well as an online presence, and some newer brokers have even moved completely into the app domain. That approach can have some drawbacks, especially for a swing trader. As a swing trader having a desktop computer is going to be an important part of your trading activities. At least right now, mobile apps don't seem to offer quite the same power.

Educational Tools

Some brokers go above and beyond and offer educational tools as well as a trading platform. If you are a new trader, that can be a very useful thing for you to have access to. Educational tools often take the form of video courses, but some platforms even offer simulated trading, which means you can practice making trades – using the real stock market – without investing actual money. The simulator will let you see how your trade works out and learn from the experience without risking a dime of money. That might be overkill for some people who are anxious actually to get active with trading, but for others who have a lot more patience, that can be useful.

Conclusion

I hope you have thoroughly enjoyed this book and congratulate you for making it to the very end!

Swing trading can be a fun and very lucrative way to make a living off the stock market. While it's slower paced than day trading, it does require that you have some tolerance for risk, that you're willing to do technical analysis of the stock market and understand what you're doing, and that you use sound judgment and don't "risk it all" for the sake of a single trade.

If you follow the principles outlined in this book, you are on your way to becoming a successful swing trader and I hope that you have found the presentation in this book to be helpful, practical, and useful.

Your education should not end here. You should read as many books as possible, and watch YouTube videos on the topic. You should also sign up for one or more official courses on swing trading so that you can thoroughly understand the fundamentals. I also recommend using a "practice" stock market simulator that some brokerages offer so that you can get your feet wet without actually risking capital. While doing all of these things may not seem appealing for those who are anxious to jump in, the more preparation that you put in, the more likely that you are going to earn profits and do well over the long term.

Think of swing trading as a business, and that will help ensure your success. Owning a business means you take reasonable risks and guard your capital. We have discussed ways to do that in the book, and I hope that you don't give in to all the common mistakes made by beginners. It can be too easy to give into emotion when trading on the stock market and large amounts of money are on the line. Don't fall prey to that temptation.

I wish the best of luck to everyone who read this book. Happy Trading!

From the same Author:

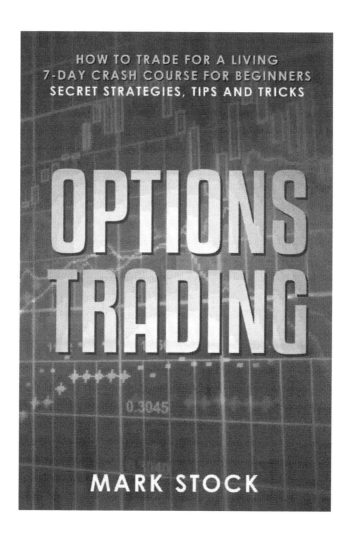

HOW TO TRADE FOR A LIVING
7-DAY CRASH COURSE FOR BEGINNERS
SECRET STRATEGIES, TIPS AND TRICKS

OPTIONS TRADING

0.3045

MARK STOCK

CURRENCY TRADING MADE SIMPLE

THE ULTIMATE FOREX TRADING GUIDE FOR BEGINNERS

SECRET STRATEGIES, TIPS AND TRICKS

FOREX TRADING

MARK STOCK

A COMPREHENSIVE GUIDE FOR BEGINNERS

STRATEGIES TO MAXIMIZE SHORT-TERM TRADING AND MAKE BIG PROFITS

SWING TRADING

WITH OPTIONS

MARK STOCK

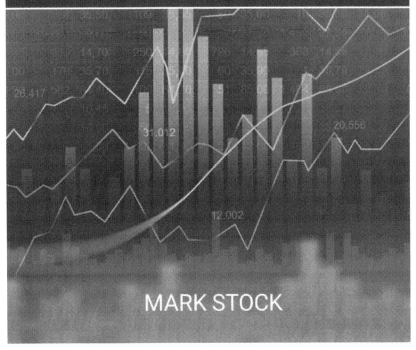

OPTIONS TRADING
FOR BEGINNERS

HOW TO TRADE FOR A LIVING
7 DAY CRASH COURSE:
SECRET STRATEGIES, TIPS AND TRICKS

MARK STOCK

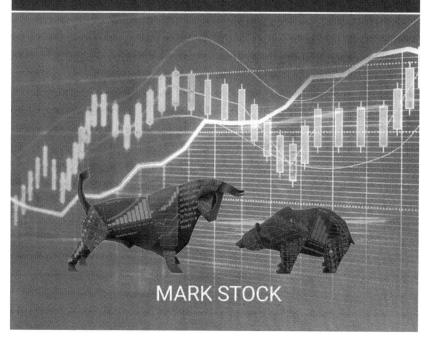

SWING TRADING
FOR BEGINNERS

A COMPREHENSIVE BEGINNER'S GUIDE
PROVEN STRATEGIES, MONEY MANAGEMENT
AND TRADING TOOLS

MARK STOCK

Made in the USA
Middletown, DE
05 September 2019